Object Management Architecture

Revision 3.0
Third Edition
June 13, 1995
Richard Mark Soley, Ph.D. (ed.)
Christopher M. Stone

John Wiley & Sons, Inc.
New York   Chichester   Brisbane   Toronto   Singapore

ISBN: 0-471-14193-3
 3 4 5 6 7 8 9 10

Preface

This document is the revised third edition of the first public document delivered by the Object Management Group (OMG). It puts forth the goals and purpose of the OMG, the structure and procedures of its Technical Committee, an Object Model for design portability, and an outine of both object technology in general and a Reference Model for the distributed application support framework being built by the OMG. It is not intended to be regarded as a complete document: it is a work-in-progress that will change as the OMG develops interface standards and specifications.

This manual is the result of the effort of scores of talented individuals from the OMG member companies and the OMG staff itself. In particular, the following people, listed alphabetically, were instrumental in completing portions of this manual, including the original draft:

William Andreas (HyperDesk Inc.)
Dr. Gerald Barber (Aldus, Inc.)
Ian Fuller (Hewlett-Packard)
Andrew Hutt (ICL)
Bill Kent (Hewlett-Packard)
Michael Kilian (Digital)
Matt Koehler (Sun Microsystems)
Jan te Kiefte (Philips Telecommunications)
Mike Mathews (Hewlett-Packard)

Gerhard Muller (Siemens Nixdorf GmbH)
Pat O'Brien (Digital)
Lee Scheffler (Constellation Software)
John Schwartz (Mentor Graphics)
Doug Smith (Hewlett-Packard)
Alan Snyder (SunSoft)
Dr. Richard Soley (OMG)
Christopher Stone (OMG)
Craig Thompson (Texas Instruments, Inc.)

This abstract, though complex, document would not have been possible without the splendid spirit of consensus among the OMG corporate members. We would like to thank all those member representatives actively involved in the OMG, and in particular all those who took the time to help with the design and production of this document.

Richard Mark Soley, Ph.D.
Christopher M. Stone
Framingham, Massachusetts USA
First Edition, September 1990
Second Edition, September 1992
Third Edition, June 1995

Contents

CHAPTER 4   *Core Object Model*   **45**

CHAPTER 1

Introduction

1.1 The OMG Vision

The CPU as an island, contained and valuable in itself, is dying in the nineties. The next paradigm of computing is distributed or cooperative computing. This is driven by the very real demands of corporations recognizing information as an asset, perhaps their most important asset.

To make use of information effectively, it must be accurate and accessible across the department, even across the world. This means that CPUs must be intimately linked to the networks of the world and be capable of freely passing and receiving information, not hidden behind glass and cooling ducts or the complexities of the software that drives them.

1.1.1 Current Problems

The major hurdles in entering this new world are provided by software: the time to develop it, the ability to maintain and enhance it, the limits on how complex a given program can be in order to be profitably produced and sold, and the time it takes to learn to use it. This leads to the major issue facing corporate information systems today: the quality, cost, and lack of interoperability of software. While hardware costs are plummeting, software expenses are rising.

As information systems attain strategic importance and represent the key competitive edge to the industry leaders, the cost of inaccuracies or delayed implementations is attenuating entire MIS departments. As systems departments require information among a diversity of inhouse, brought-in, supplier, customer, and commercial applications, those applications become increasingly difficult and complex.

1.1.2 The OMG Solution

The Object Management Group (OMG) was formed to help reduce complexity, lower costs, and hasten the introduction of new software applications. The OMG plans to accomplish this through the introduction of an architectural framework with supporting detailed interface specifications. These specifications will drive the industry towards interoperable, reusable, portable software components based on standard object-oriented interfaces.

The OMG is an international trade association incorporated as a non-profit in the United States. The OMG receives funding on a yearly dues basis from its diverse membership of more than 470 corporations. The OMG is headquartered in Framingham, Massachusetts, and has marketing offices in Frankfurt, Germany; Tokyo, Japan; and Hounslow, England. The OMG also sponsors the world's largest exhibition and conference on object technology, Object World. The mission of the OMG is as follows:

- The Object Management Group is dedicated to maximizing the portability, reusability, and interoperability of software. The OMG is the leading worldwide organization dedicated to producing a framework and specifications for commercially available object-oriented environments.

- The Object Management Group provides a Reference Architecture with terms and definitions upon which all specifications are based. Implementations of these specifications will be made available under fair and equitable terms and conditions. The OMG will create industry standards for commercially available object-oriented systems by focusing on Distributed Applications, Distributed Services, and Common Facilities.

- The OMG provides an open forum for industry discussion, education, and promotion of OMG-endorsed object technology. The OMG coordinates its activities with related organizations and acts as a technology/marketing center for object-oriented software.

The OMG defines the object management paradigm as the ability to encapsulate data and methods for software development. This models the "real world" through representation of program components called "objects." This representation results in faster application development, easier maintenance, reduced program complexity, and reusable components. A central benefit of an object-oriented system is its ability to grow in functionality through the extension of existing components and the addition of new objects to the system.

The software concept of "objects," as incorporated into the technology of the Object Management Group, will provide solutions to the software complexities of the 1990s. Object-oriented architectures will allow applications acquired from different sources and installed on different systems to freely exchange information. Software "objects" will mirror the real world business objects they support, in the sense that the architect's blueprint mirror a building. The OMG envisions a day where users of software start up applications as they start up their cars, with no more concern about the underlying structure of the objects they manipulate than the driver has about the molecular construction of gasoline.

1.2 Goals of the OMG

The members of the Object Management Group have a shared goal of developing and using integrated software systems. These systems should be built using a methodology that supports modular production of software; encourages reuse of code; allows useful integration across lines of developers, operating systems and hardware; and enhances long-range maintenance of that code. Members of the OMG believe that the object-oriented approach to software construction best supports their goals.

Object orientation, at both the programming language and applications environment levels, provides a terrific boost in programmer productivity, and greatly lends itself to the production of integrated software systems. While not necessarily promoting faster programming, object technology allows you to construct more with less code. This is partly due to the naturalness of the approach, and also to its rigorous requirement for interface specification. The only thing missing is a set of standard interfaces for interoperable software components. This is the mission of the OMG.

Member companies join the OMG because they see themselves in a position to capitalize on a decade's work in object-oriented development by constructing a real system based on a vision of a distributed object-oriented architecture for application development. A major goal is to define a living, evolving standard with realized parts, so that applications developers can deliver their applications with off-the-shelf components for common facilities like object storage, class structure, peripheral interface, user interface, etc. The function of the OMG is then to promulgate the standard specifications throughout the international industry, and to foster the development of tools and software components compliant with the standard.

1.3 The OMG Process

The OMG Board of Directors approves the standard by explicit vote on a technology-by-technology basis. The OMG Board of Directors bases its decisions on both business and technical merit. As portions of the reference model are proposed to be filled by various vendors' software specifications, the standard grows. The purpose of the OMG Technical Committee (TC) is to provide technical guidance and recommendations to the Board in making these technology decisions. An end-user special interest group likewise guides the Board toward decisions in the best interests of technology users.

The TC is composed of representatives of all OMG member companies (Corporate, Associate, and End User), with similar voting provisions to the Board's voting structure. It is operated by a Vice President of Technology, working full-time for the OMG (as opposed to being employed by a member company). The TC operates in a Request for Proposal (RFP) mode, requesting technology to fill open portions of the reference model from the international industry. (This document lays the groundwork for technology response to our Requests for Proposals and subsequent adoption of specifications.) The responses to an RFP, taken within a specific response period, are evaluated by a Task Force of the Technical Committee. Then, the full TC votes on a recommendation to the Board for approval of the proposed addition to the standard. Once a technology specification (not source code or product) has been adopted, it is promulgated by the OMG to the industry through a variety of distribution channels. The specifications that are currently promulgated by the OMG are listed in "Associated Documents" on page 13.

There also exists a somewhat faster model for adopting standards, one that is based on Requests for Public Comment (RFC).

For more information about the RFC and RFP processes, refer to Appendix B.

1.4 Benefits of Object Management

As previously mentioned, the technological approach of object technology (or object orientation) was chosen by the OMG founders not for its own sake, but in order to attain a set of end user goals. End users benefit in a number of ways from the object-oriented approach to application construction:

- An object-oriented user interface has many advantages over more traditional user interfaces. In an object-oriented user interface, Application Objects (computer simulated representations of real world objects) are presented to end users as objects that can be manipulated in a way that is similar to the manipulation of the real world objects. Examples of such object-oriented user interfaces are realized in systems such as Xerox Star, Apple Macintosh, NeXTStep from NeXT Computer, OSF Motif and HP NewWave, and to a limited degree, Microsoft Windows. CAD systems are also a good example in which components of a design can be manipulated in a way similar to the manipulation of real components.

  This results in a reduced learning curve and common "look and feel" to multiple applications. It is easier to see and point than to remember and type.

- A more indirect end-user benefit of object-oriented applications, provided that they cooperate according to some standard, is that independently developed general purpose applications can be combined in a user-specific way. It is the OMG's central purpose to create a standard that realizes interoperability between independently developed applications across heterogeneous networks of computers.

  This means that multiple software programs appear as "one" to the user of information no matter where they reside.

- Common functionality in different applications (such as storage and retrieval of objects, mailing of objects, printing of objects, creation and deletion of objects, or help and computer-based training) is realized by common shared objects leading to a uniform and consistent user interface.

  Sharing of information drastically reduces documentation redundancy. Consistent access across multiple applications allows for increased focus on application creation rather than application education.

- Transition to object-oriented application technology does not make existing applications obsolete. Existing applications can be embedded (with different levels of integration) in an object-oriented environment.

Pragmatic migration of existing applications gives users control over their computing resources, and how quickly these resources change.

Likewise, application developers benefit from object technology and object-oriented standards. These benefits fall into two categories:

- Through encapsulation of object data (making data accessible only in a way controlled by the software that implements the object) applications are built in a truly modular fashion, preventing unintended interference. In addition, it is possible to build applications in an incremental way, preserving correctness during the development process.

- Reuse of existing components. Specifically, when the OMG standard is in effect, thereby standardizing interaction between independently developed applications (and application components), cost and lead time can be saved by making use of existing implementations of object classes.

In developing standards, the OMG keeps these benefits of object orientation in mind, together with a set of overall goals:

- Heterogeneity. Integration of applications and facilities must be available across heterogeneous networks of systems independent of networking transports and operating systems.

- Customization options. Common Facilities must be customizable in order to meet specific end-user or organizational requirements and preferences.

- Scope. The scope of OMG adopted technology is characterized by both work group support and mission critical applications.

- Management and control. Issues such as security, recovery, inter-ruptibility, auditing, and performance are examined.

- Internationalization. As the OMG is itself an international group, the standard reflects built-in support for internationalization of software.

- Technical standards. Standards to meet these user goals are the central goal of the OMG, as well as the content of this manual.

1.5 Summary of the OMA Guide

Chapter 2 provides an overview of the Object Management Architecture. The overview describes the problems that the OMG seeks to solve. The OMG believes that by working together with its members and the industry as a whole we can all deliver high-quality software in a timely manner. This will obviate the need for programmers to produce different versions of their applications across multiple computing environments. For users, this means greater flexibility to choose software that solves their problems, not because it's the only one that "runs" on their system.

Chapter 3 details technical objectives for the standard itself, as well as requirements on technology proposed for adoption by the OMG.

Chapter 4 represents a model of common object semantics. The common semantics characterize objects that exist in an OMA-compliant system. This chapter describes a core set of requirements that must be supported in any system that complies with the Core Object Model standard. It builds a common lexicon for OMG Technical Committee members and the industry to discuss proposed technologies. Thus, this chapter becomes the dictionary used by members proposing technology to the OMG. (Its contents are condensed in a glossary format in Appendix A.)

Chapter 5 presents the OMG's Reference Model. Although OMG products are built from extant products, there needs to be a central design core to ensure interoperability, code reusability, portability, and heterogeneous extensibility. In addition, companies considering proposing technology to the OMG require a central design guideline to understand the system structure that the OMG is building. This chapter lays these ground rules, giving the overall abstract structure of an application and the major interfaces it needs to operate. It includes API definitions, data exchange interfaces, and so forth. This chapter is also the source of industry Requests for Information (RFIs) and Requests for Proposal (RFPs) and Request for Comment (RFC) from the OMG Technical Committee, and the basis for any certification efforts that may evolve.

Appendix A is a glossary of terms. Appendix B, "Policies and Procedures," explains the rules that govern the OMG Technical Committee. The policies and procedures were adopted on January 3, 1990 and amended through April 1995.

1.5.1 Associated Documents

In addition to this book, the OMG offers the following specifications:

- *CORBA: Common Object Request Broker Architecture and Specification* contains the architecture and specifications for the Common Object Request Broker.

- *CORBAservices: Common Object Services Specification* contains specifications for the object services.

- *CORBAfacilities: Common Facilities* will contain specifications for Common Facilities; it is currently scheduled for publication in mid-1995.

The OMG collects information for each specification by issuing Requests for Information, Requests for Proposals, and Requests for

Comment and, with its membership, evaluating the responses. Specifications are adopted as standards only when representatives of the OMG membership accept them as such by vote.

To obtain these or other OMG publications, contact the Object Management Group, Inc., at:

> OMG Headquarters
> 492 Old Connecticut Path
> Framingham, MA 01701
> USA
> Tel: +1-508-820-4300
> pubs@omg.org
> http://www.omg.org

1.6 Conclusion

In the ideal sense, computing should be viewed by the users as "my" world, with no artificial barriers of operating system, hardware architecture, network compatibility, or application incompatibility.

Software, in essence, is an art form expressed in the past through procedural construction that has never really modeled the "real" world. The real world approach is quite simply a commodity approach where software is designed and built from logical components, snapped together with "requests" where the sum of the parts is equal to, and many times greater than, the whole.

The reality of distributed network computing and object-oriented products is here. The job now is to develop standardization for tools and applications that reduce the effort it takes to build the applications of tomorrow. The OMG plays a valuable role as a catalyst for progress which can only be achieved through cooperation among industry participants.

Over time, the use of object oriented concepts will make this "ideal" computing environment a reality. It is the gateway through which even the most compuphobic person can pass. It has the potential to enable users to control their computing environment, rather than being controlled by its limitations. Please join with us to realize this vision.

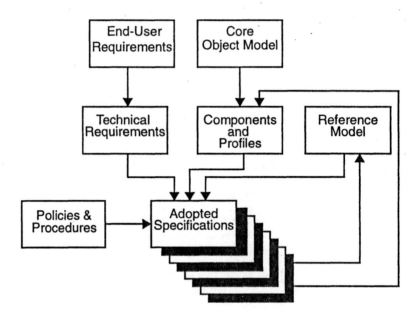

Figure 1-1   Structure of the OMA Guide

CHAPTER 2

Overview

2.1 Introduction

This chapter uses typical problems and their OMG solutions to describe what the OMG's Object Management Architecture tries to achieve. The examples in this chapter should put the rest of the guide in perspective and help the user to appreciate the proposed technology as outlined in the following chapters.

This chapter makes several assumptions: first, that the OMG's Object Management Architecture is mature; second, that conforming platforms and applications are abundant; and third, that the examples, taken from the mechanical CAD world, apply to other application areas as well.

2.2 The Advantages of OMA for System Vendors

Situation: A supplier of CAD workstations has, on the basis of hardware and a CAD-M application, a good position in the CAD-M market.

Problem 1: A large customer requires that the manuals related to his design be created on another supplier's publishing workstations, directly accessing the design information.

Solution: With the OMG's Object Management Architecture in place, the CAD-M design objects are stored on a database server. These objects are accessed by CAD application functions (methods) for drawing, parts explosion, and others. The new documentation requirements can be implemented by connecting the publishing equipment to the CAD network. A multimedia editor runs on the publishing workstations and addresses the CAD-M design objects to generate the drawings to be included in the documentation. Some editing is of course required: an illustration in a manual usually takes a different format than a design drawing. The design objects may require a method to generate a representation in a format compatible with the publishing software, since there are many standards in the CAD world.

Equipment as well as software from different sources can interoperate. Substantial functional extensions can be made by applying a minimum of glue between nonrelated but existing applications. Software is reusable and extensible.

Problem 2: A major competitor expands its product with support for circuit board design. To be competitive, the system vendor must port software supplied by a leading OEM.

Solution: The solution of the second problem is even simpler: if the system vendor's hardware and systems software is indeed a platform supported by the Object Management Architecture and the circuit board design application conforms to the Object Management Architecture, the porting of the circuit board design application is straightforward and the system vendor as well as the OEM software supplier can enjoy a productive OEM contract. Applications written in conformance with the Object Management Architecture are portable. Translating these technical opportunities in business terms, it means that the system vendor can profit from the OMG's Object Management Architecture due to:

- Reduced initial cost to make new functionality available (alternatively, more functionality offered to the customers at the same cost) since existing software (from the System Vendor or from OEM sources) can easily be integrated.

- Early availability of a larger number of functions, leading to an extension of the market size.

2.3 The Advantages of OMA for Independent Software Vendors

Situation: An independent software vendor (ISV) has a position in stress analysis of mechanical parts.

Problem: The ISV wants to extend the functionality with software for the simulation of dynamic behavior of mechanical designs. The target is a set of existing CAD-M platforms.

Solution: Object Management Architecture is not magic: complex applications (like simulation of dynamic behavior of mechanical designs) require hard work. However, OMG's technology allows the ISV in this example to concentrate on the essentials: the complexity of simulation.

The Object Management Architecture comes with standardized Object Services (for application controlled management of objects) and a set of Common Facilities, in this case, helping to visualize the results of the simulation.

When used in a CAD-M environment that provides methods for parts explosion and retrieval of design data, OMG technology results in extended end-user functionality while conserving the existing design environment.

Since the simulation of dynamic behavior may involve heavy number crunching, calculations can be delegated to a dedicated server, providing the necessary megaflops, and leaving the CAD workstation resources free for interactive design work.

The Object Management Architecture improves productivity by reusing existing parts (and thus focusing on essentials). Object-oriented software design using the standard components of the Object Management Architecture imposes a design philosophy that leads to less iteration during the design phase. Object Management Architecture provides transparency over heterogeneous networks, allowing specific tasks to be delegated to specific machines.

2.4 The Advantages of OMA for End Users

Situation: A central CAD department of a pump factory supplying a large variety of pumping equipment.

Problem: The management of the central CAD department of the pump factory gets the following tasks:

- Fine-tune the design of a series of high-precision pumps. A CAD-M system is available but fine-tuning requires stress analysis and simulation of dynamic behavior of the moving parts in the pump's design.

- Refine reporting of design costs to reflect the cost per product line. The accounting department is equipped with PC workstations connected to the factory's LAN. Reporting from accounting is based on regular word processing and spreadsheet applications.

- Propose, in cooperation with the documentation department, an improved procedure for the production of manufacturing and service documentation. The documentation department uses desktop publishing equipment, connected to the factory's LAN. The supplier of the CAD equipment has a stress analysis package in its catalogue and is able to install that package on the current equipment. (Refer to "The Advantages of OMA for System Vendors," on page 18.) The same supplier has recently announced the availability of an extension allowing simulation of dynamic behavior of mechanical designs. A contact with the ISV supplying that software indicates that the necessary vibration analysis can indeed be done but will require more number-crunching capacity than is currently available.

Solution: The pump factory's computer consultant indicates how the classes of the CAD-M package can be extended with an automatic time-stamp facility. Each week, the collection of time stamps is put into a spreadsheet format and is sent to Accounting. The implementation work needed is assigned to a software house specializing in Object Management Architecture–conforming software.

Another extension to the CAD-M classes is an option to extract drawings from the CAD-M object database in a format required by the desktop publishing software. The documentation department gets (read-only) access to released design objects in the database of the CAD department.

For the end user, standardized interfaces for object-oriented application software provide the option of extensibility of existing software. In addition, through encapsulation of non-conforming applications (like the spreadsheet package of Accounting), the transition to the new technology can be a gradual one. The productivity of an organization can be improved through exploitation of the interoperability of conforming software over heterogeneous networks. In addition, the object-oriented approach to application software guarantees an intuitive user interface: computer-simulated objects correspond with real world objects, whether they are the blades of a pump, a pump's service manuals, or weekly reports on the time spent on a specific design. Standardization of object-oriented technology creates uniformity and consistency over different and independently developed applications.

2.5   Object Management Architecture

The Object Request Broker component of the Object Management Architecture is the communications heart of the standard. This is referred to commercially as CORBA (Common Object Request Broker Architecture). It provides an infrastructure allowing objects to communicate, independent of the specific platforms and techniques used to implement the addressed objects. The Object Request Broker component will guarantee portability and interoperability of objects over a network of heterogeneous system. Specifications for the Common Object Request Broker are contained in *CORBA:Common Object Request Broker Architecture and Specification.*

The Object Services component standardizes the life cycle management of objects. Functions are provided to create objects (the Object Factory), to control access to objects, to keep track of relocated objects and to consistently maintain the relationship between groups of objects. The Object Service components provide the generic environment in which single objects can perform their tasks. Standardization of Object Services leads to consistency over different applications and improved productivity for the developer. Specifications for the Object Services that have been adopted as standards by the OMG are contained in *CORBAservices: Common Object Services Specifications.*

The Common Facilities component provides a set of generic application functions that can be configured to the requirements of a specific configuration. Examples are printing facilities, database facilities, and electronic mail facilities. Standardization leads to uniformity in generic operations and to options for end users to configure their configurations (as opposed to configuring individual applications).

The Application Objects part of the architecture represents those application objects performing specific tasks for users. One application is typically built from a large number of basic object classes, partly specific for the application, partly from the set of Common Facilities. New classes of application objects can be built by modification of existing classes through generalization or specialization of existing classes (inheritance) as provided by Object Services. The multi-object class approach to application development leads to improved productivity for the developer and to options for end users to combine and configure their applications.

Chapter 5 contains more information about the Object Request Broker, Object Services, Common Facilities, and Application Objects.

CHAPTER 3

Technical Objectives

3.1 Purpose and Scope

This chapter describes the technical objectives of the OMG. The OMG intends to achieve these objectives by adopting technology within the overall framework of the OMG's Object Management Architecture (see Chapter 5). While the OMG is seeking to adopt and standardize the interface and protocol specifications identified by the OMA, sponsored technology that supports the proposed interfaces and protocols must satisfy the OMG's Technical Objectives.

The objectives are expressed from the point of view of a developer of an application that uses the services provided by the OMA. The objectives cover the total capabilities of the OMA. A given objective might therefore be satisfied or achieved by a combination of OMA elements.

3.2 Use in RFI/RFP Process

The OMA Reference Model partitions the OMG problem space into practical high-level architectural components for which RFIs or RFPs may be issued. The Reference Model enables technology proposers to understand how to present and position their proposals. The OMG Object Model defines the theoretical basis that proposed technology should conform to or support, as well as a glossary of terms to provide a uniformity of concepts.

The OMG Technical Objectives describe the characteristics and capabilities of the technology whose interface and protocol specifications the OMG is interested in adopting, without over-constraining the possible design solutions. Individual RFI/RFPs may further define specific requirements on proposed technology derived from the Technical Objectives.

Vendors are expected to propose technologies positioned within the Reference Model components that, when taken together, achieve the OMG's Technical Objectives. They are expected to respond to each specific objective or requirement and describe the capabilities of their proposed technology that address or satisfy it. An individual vendor may not however be able to address all the objectives. In this case, the proposer must explain the supporting or complementary technology required for a total solution.

Vendors should also explain the scalability of their proposed technology, justifying the viability of implementations for single machines, multi-machine client-server configurations, fully distributed networks of heterogeneous machines, and communicating networks that employ different "interoperability profiles."

The objectives are arranged into primary and secondary categories (labeled explicitly). The OMG intends to place the most emphasis on technology that achieves the primary objectives.

For more information about the RFI and RFP, refer to "Steps to Technology Adoption," on page 138.

3.2.1 Use in RFC Process

In order to allow "fast-track" adoption of an interface, for which a Corporate member has an acceptable commercially available implementation with no competition, there is a second path to technology adoption that operates in parallel and instead of the Request for Proposals procedure.

Any Corporate member with technology that meets the following criteria may use an RFC to make an unsolicited submission of that technology to the relevant TFC:

- Relevant to a current Task Force adoption plan
- Conformance with all applicable OMG-adopted technologies
- Available in a commercially available implementation

For more information about the RFC, refer to "Fast-Track Request for Comments Procedure," on page 147.

3.3 Overall Technical Goal of the OMG

The overall technical goal of the OMG is to adopt interface and protocol specifications that define an object management architecture; the architecture must support interoperable applications that are based on distributed, interoperating objects. The specifications are to be based on existing technology that demonstrably satisfies the OMG's Technical Objectives. These objectives apply both to individual implementations of OMG-adopted technologies and to cooperating (interoperating) collections of such objects.

3.4 Detailed Technical Objectives

3.4.1 Conform to the OMG Object Model.

Proposed technology should define and support an Object Model that conforms to the OMG Object Model. Specifically, the following should be supported:

3.4.1.1 Inheritance of interface (i.e., conformance of interface types).

3.4.1.2 Inheritance of implementation (secondary).

3.4.1.3 A program or process should be able to define and execute one or more methods.

3.4.1.4 The methods of an object may be defined and executed in one or more programs or processes.

3.4.2 Distribute objects transparently.

A client object using a server object through its interface should be independent of the server object's:

3.4.2.1 Location—the physical location of the object's methods and associated state.

3.4.2.2 Access path—the path between the client and server objects.

3.4.2.3 Relocation—the movement of the data or methods of the object to new locations.

If object relocation is supported (i.e., the moving of object data or methods to new locations), it should not require that a client object be modified in order to use the relocated server object. (Note that support for object relocation itself is a secondary objective.)

3.4.2.4 Representation—the format of the data and methods associated with the object.

The various choices for storing data or computing it, and what actual data types are stored and in what combinations, should be purely an implementation matter. If the internal representation of an object is changed, this should not affect its interface or client behavior.

3.4.2.5 Communication mechanism—how communication with the process that is performing a request is effected.

A number of different interprocess communication mechanisms may be simultaneously in use within a particular local or distributed object management infrastructure. Which mechanisms are being used at any given time to communicate object requests may depend on the relative locations of communicating processes and other relevant characteristics. A client object should be able to send requests to a server object without needing to be aware of the specific underlying communications mechanisms employed or the specific protocols used.

3.4.2.6 Invocation mechanism—how methods associated with the object are executed.

Different operating systems supply different models and mechanisms for controlling computer processes (e.g., dynamically linked libraries and parent/child processes). Methods rely on these mechanisms for their operation. A client process should not need to be aware of the mechanisms in use by a server object's methods, nor should the client operation be affected by a change in the mechanism for any method.

3.4.2.7 Storage mechanisms—how the data and methods of the object are stored and managed.

3.4.2.8 Machine type—the computer hardware architecture on which the object's methods are executed.

3.4.2.9 Operating system—the basic software operating environment supporting the method execution of the object.

3.4.2.10 Programming language—the programming languages in which the methods of the object are implemented.

3.4.2.11 Security mechanism—the specific mechanism in force to control access to the object.

The security mechanism used to control access to a server object should not affect the interface of the object.

Changes in any of the above should not require a client to be recompiled, relinked, or reloaded in order to maintain the distribution transparency of the server object.

3.4.3 Consider performance for local and remote server object requests.

Criteria for evaluation shall include:

3.4.3.1 Scalability—the effect on request processing times as the numbers of objects accessible to a client increases and the number of requests handled increases.

3.4.3.2 Method invocation time—the overhead associated with the first and subsequent requests to local and remote objects and the corresponding responses.

3.4.3.3 Storage overhead—the storage associated with maintaining information about objects.

3.4.3.4 Resource consumption—the run-time storage, memory, and processing requirements.

3.4.3.5 Parallelism—the degree of support for concurrent execution.

3.4.3.6   Throughput—the capacity to handle significant numbers of simultaneous requests and responses.

3.4.4 Objects are extensible and dynamic in nature.

It should be possible to make changes dynamically to the implementation of objects without affecting other objects, whether or not they are clients of the changed objects. Such changes should not require other objects to be recompiled, relinked, or reloaded; nor should it require the shutdown of the environment, in at least the following cases:

3.4.4.1   Adding new implementations (e.g., new classes) should not affect existing objects.

3.4.4.2   Replacing implementations where the interface is not changed. Any change to the implementation of an object that does not change its object interface should not affect other objects. In specific cases, this might include:

- Adding, replacing, and deleting methods or data structures.

- Changing the type of an attribute or method.

- Renaming classes, attributes, and methods.

- Changing the class relationship structure (i.e., object inheritance) including changing which superclass(es) do or do not provide inherited components.

3.4.4.3   Replacing implementations where the interface is changed (secondary).

To accommodate changes to the implementation of an object that cause changes to its interface, a mechanism should be provided (e.g., based on versioning) such that existing objects can continue to use older implementations. Alternatively, a dynamic upgrade facility might allow existing objects to correctly use the new interface.

3.4.4.4   Changing the location of implementations (secondary).

Changes to the physical location of any part of the implementation of an object (e.g., moving methods, attributes, or the storage of object relationships) should not affect other objects.

Note that non-dynamic changes may also be supported, particularly if such support provides tangible benefits such as higher performance or better utilization of storage capabilities.

3.4.5 *Provide a naming system that supports multiple naming contexts.*

A naming system allows names to be mapped to objects in a context. It should be possible to support different naming conventions and policies. Contexts should support mapping to different name spaces.

The architecture should facilitate:

3.4.5.1   Name spaces in which objects can be named unambiguously. An object can have more than one name. The names associated with an object may change over time and can therefore be considered attributes of an object. The values (e.g., objects) to which the names are mapped can also change.

3.4.5.2   Object handles. The notion of an object handle that is unique for an object is supported. The purpose of a handle is to identify an object uniquely regardless of its other names.

3.4.5.3   Efficient references to objects. This may be inherent in the support for object names or handles.

3.4.6 Queries are based on object names, attributes, and relationships with other objects.

In addition, support should be provided for queries on:

3.4.6.1   Implementation information including class and method.

3.4.6.2   Type information.

3.4.6.3   Interface information for any given object.

3.4.6.4   Naming system data.

3.4.7 Support discretionary access control of objects.

Discretionary access control means that access control can be set by an object's owner and cannot normally be circumvented.

3.4.7.1   Access controls should be able to be set on objects controlled by a server (e.g., which clients can make what requests to the object).

To provide complete data access control, an object's data should not normally be accessible by any means other than the methods of its class.

3.4.7.2   Such access control should also be provided for metaobject data including implementation and interface information, and naming system data.

3.4.7.3   Mandatory access control, such as that specified by national defense administrations, may also be supported (secondary).

Note that this requirement implies some form of client-server authentication scheme if complete reliability is to be guaranteed.

3.4.8 Provide concurrency control for objects.

When necessary, an object must be able to mediate simultaneous accesses by one or more client objects so that it remains consistent and coherent. For example, an object may use locking so that it is unavailable while data modification is in progress. The concurrency control mechanism may be provided as part of the environment (e.g., based on automatic versioning) or be provided by specific object implementations.

The concurrency control mechanism should, at a minimum, support:

3.4.8.1   Implicit concurrency control. Server objects are responsible for mediating access to themselves. Stated conversely, client objects should not need to perform explicit actions to insure the consistency of the objects they access.

3.4.8.2   A parallelism policy. The mechanism should minimize the unavailability of a server object due to its use by another client object. For example, the concurrency control mechanism could queue requests, it could support parallel threads of execution, or it could support locking of only affected sub-objects or sub-components.

3.4.8.3   Different types of use. The mechanism should distinguish different types of use where this is advantageous. For example, the mechanism may distinguish read access and write accesses so that read requests can be processed simultaneously.

3.4.8.4   Recovery from abnormal conditions. The mechanism must be able to detect abnormal conditions such as the unexpected failure of a client object and recover such that no server object is left in a state in which it cannot process new requests.

3.4.9 Provide transactions for the purpose of atomically committing the result of an operation or sequence of operations on distributed objects.

This includes support for:

3.4.9.1   Atomic sequences of operations that take place over a short period of time for which consistency is required (i.e., short transactions).

3.4.9.2   Atomic sequences of operations that may together last over a significant period of time but consisting of parts that can be separately committed in stages (i.e., long transactions) (secondary).

3.4.10 Provide robust operation and a high level of availability.

The environment should be able to detect inconsistencies resulting from abnormal conditions and terminations and gracefully recover within an acceptable period of time.

This includes support for:

3.4.10.1 Notification to client objects of abnormal terminations (e.g., failure of request delivery or method invocation).

3.4.10.2 Recovery back to a consistent state. This may require application cooperation or be automatic (secondary).

3.4.11 Provide support for the versioning of objects.

In addition, provides support for:

3.4.11.1 Versioning of classes with existing instances (secondary).

This includes the ability to install a new version of a class without affecting existing instances, and, when old instances are run, ensuring that they use the old version of their class.

3.4.12 Provide support for the notification of events to interested objects.

A notification mechanism should be supported such that the object that triggers an event need not know the set of objects that are interested in receiving notification of the occurrence of that event.

This includes support for an object to:

3.4.12.1 Register interest in an event.

3.4.12.2 Define and trigger events.

3.4.12.3 Receive notification of events in the same way as normal requests are received.

3.4.13 Provide support for inter-object semantic relationships

by holding object references within other objects.

3.4.14 Provide an application programming interface for all object management functions and capabilities with, as a minimum, a C binding.

3.4.15 Require minimal administration of the environment and facilitates management of the object base.

In particular:

3.4.15.1 The environment should be self-administrating as far as possible but, where this is not feasible, should support distributed (non-centralized) administration.

3.4.15.2 Backups of all or part of the object base should be able to be incremental with only short interruptions in the availability of objects.

3.4.15.3 Restoration of objects from backups should be possible in such a way that non-restored objects (that may contain references to the restored objects) continue to work (secondary).

3.4.16 Support application internationalization.

Internationalization is the ability of an application to carry out interaction with users in their language and according to their preferences (e.g., culturally defined).

This includes support for application customization with respect to:

3.4.16.1 The language used at the user interface, for example, extended Latin character sets, non-Latin character sets (secondary), and languages that are not written from left to right (secondary).

3.4.16.2 Different culturally defined conventions (e.g., collating sequences, date and time notation, currency symbols, street address formats, postal codes, telephone numbers, titles).

3.4.16.3 Dynamic switching between different languages and conventions used at the user interface (e.g., for point-of-sale or teller applications in multilingual or multicultural societies) (secondary).

3.4.17 Conform to pertinent industry standards.

In general, technology should conform to broadly accepted standards including:

- X/Open endorsed standards
- POSIX
- ANSI C
- Relevant parts of ISO RM-ODP standards
- Other relevant ISO standards

Areas where no standard exists or where there are competing standards shall be evaluated on a case-by-case basis. The rationale for utilizing specific standards in this case should be given.

To achieve inter-domain application interoperability, the Object Request Broker (ORB) component of the OMG's Object Management Architecture (OMA) must be based on a set of underlying layers addressing such things as physical and logical connectivity and the common low-level protocol for communication. Proposed ORB specifications and protocols must allow implementations that are based on different "interoperability profiles." An interoperability profile defines the standards that apply to these underlying layers.

The set of standards to which a particular ORB implementation conforms (and the OMA-specific protocols to be used) forms the interoperability profile for that implementation. Different implementations of the ORB may use different profiles. If two ORB implementations use the same interoperability profile, then application interoperability can take place between them (by definition).

Rather than mandate a single profile, the OMG intends to focus on the standardization of the application interface to the OMA and allow the marketplace (and other standards organizations) to decide on favored interoperability profiles for the underlying layers.

CHAPTER 4

Core Object Model

There are many different object models in existence. To date, the OMG has formalized two object models: the Core Object Model and the CORBA profile. (The CORBA profile is described in *CORBA: Common Object Request Broker Specification and Architecture.*) The Core Object Model was first defined in 1992, and revised in 1995.

This chapter describes the Core Object Model, which is the formal model specifying the features that all OMA-compliant object systems should support. It describes:

- The underlying ideas of an object model, which provide a context for the Core Object Model

- The goals (and non-goals) of the Core Object Model

- The common object semantics of the Core Object Model, including information about objects, operations, non-object types, types, interfaces, and inheritance

- The relationship between CORBA and the Core Object Model

4.1 Context of the Core Object Model

An object model, as defined by the OMG, is based on the basic ideas shown in Figure 4-1. These fundamental ideas are:

- **All object oriented concepts,** which include the larger world of object-oriented notions, including such concepts as object, attribute, inheritance, and so forth.

- **The Core Object Model** is a set of concepts that are commonly agreed upon as defining object-based software. The Core Object Model is the highest level of an object model.

- **A component** introduces a further set of concepts—an extension—to the Core Object Model. A component is compatible with the Core Object Model if:

- It adds but does not replace concepts.

- It does not duplicate concepts.

- It does not remove concepts.

- The concepts defined within a component should be minimal and sufficient.

Ideally, components (extensions) should be orthogonal to each other. If two components have common concepts, then these concepts could be considered as part of the Core Object Model, not as a component of the Core Object Model.

- **A profile** is some combination of the Core Object Model plus one or more components that together provide a useful set of concepts to underpin a specification or product architecture. For example, CORBA is a kind of profile.

Figure 4-1 illustrates these ideas.

4.2 Goals of the Core Object Model

The Core Object Model was designed to achieve two goals: first, the portability of applications and type libraries; and second, the interoperability of software components in a distributed, heterogeneous environment.

4.2.1 Portability

A portable system is one that has built in support for objects:

- Across different technology domains, such as programming languages, database management systems, object request brokers, and GUI

- Within the same technology domain but across different products from a wide range of system software vendors

Without such support, application developers are highly dependent on a particular vendor's system. For example, since application code is not portable across different ODBMS products, developers are tied to both the fate of the underlying system software vendor and to that vendor's ability to port the software widely. Furthermore, suppose an application depends on several software products that do not share the same basic object model–for example, an ODBMS and an OGUI. In that case, an application is much more complicated to write because it has to accommodate two object models: one in talking to the disk, the other in talking to the screen.

There are three levels of portability:

1. Design portability
2. Source code portability
3. Object code portability

The Core Object Model addresses design portability. It does not develop a syntax for an Object Definition Language (ODL), nor does it prescribe the syntactic forms for binding the Core Object Model to object programming languages (OPL) or ODBMS Object Manipulation Languages (OML). Since it stops short of defining syntax, it cannot ensure source code portability across different ODBMS, ORB, or programming language implementations. However, in defining a common semantics for the object model, it does ensure that the basic design of a large application or type library will be portable across all OMA-compliant components. Design portability is highly valuable to the user community, since the major investment in any large application is the design itself: the way the design is broken into types, the semantics of the individual types, and their relationships.

Agreement on a common semantics for the Core Object Model is also the prerequisite first step toward higher levels of portability, such as source code portability and object code portability.

4.2.2 Interoperability

Interoperability is a more ambitious, longer-term objective. It implies runtime compatibility between applications, class libraries, and the runtime systems of ODBMS, OGUI, and OPL products supplied by different vendors, running on different processors with different operating systems. The ORB is a first step in this direction. It allows invocation of operations on objects distributed around a network without regard to the networking software, operating system, or application that implements those objects. As the industry moves into implementation of ORB-based applications, however, it will become clear that a transport mechanism alone is not sufficient to provide interoperability. To make an analogy: the reason that two people can communicate by phone is their shared understanding of the semantics of a common language, not the phone line's ability to transmit sound. The phone line is a prerequisite, but alone it is insufficient for meaningful communication. Likewise, meaningful communication between distributed systems requires both an ORB (our phone line) and the Core Object Model (the basis of our commonly understood language).

Interoperability can be achieved by specifications at different levels of abstraction:

- At the lowest level are detailed syntax and protocols for making and managing requests to facilitate basic communication.

- Common representation of object formats are needed to allow for object interchange between systems/tools.

- Standard language syntax, such as SQL2 extensions or C++, are used to provide a consistent application or user interface.

- Common object semantics, defined in language-neutral fashion, are necessary to provide a uniform understanding of identity, inheritance, polymorphism, containment, query, types and classes, and so forth.

- At the highest level, domain-specific standards are used to promote correctness of interoperating applications in particular domains.

The Core Object Model currently specifies a common object semantics.

4.3 Non-Goals of the Core Object Model

Non-goals of the Core Object Model are just as important as the goals in understanding the Core Object Model.

First, the Core Object Model is **not** a meta model. It is not intended to be a model for describing or deriving other object models. It specifies one object model. A meta model that allowed the derivation of several different object models would not meet our objective of design portability. For example, a class library that was developed using an object programming language that supports one object model must usually be rewritten to be used with an object programming language that supports a different object model. Rewriting is necessary even if both object models are derived from a single meta model.

Second, the Core Object Model has not been constrained to be either a strict superset or a least common denominator of the features of existing OPLs or ODBMSs. A superset approach is not appropriate because technology domains would want to construct profiles that restrict features of the general model. Such restriction would undermine portability and interoperability, since there would be no common set of concepts for profiles to share. The least common denominator approach does not support a model that is rich enough to be useful.

Third, the Core Object Model is not intended to be the "ultimate" object model. It is intended to satisfy the modest goal of design reusability and at the same time enable the OMG and other technology groups to enhance the model to meet the needs of their respective domains. The Core Object Model, components, and profiles are intended to evolve to meet the changing requirements of these technology groups.

Finally, the Core Object Model is not meant to be another paper model done as a design exercise. The OMG's intention is that adopted technology comply with the Core Object model.

To meet these goals and non-goals, the specification for the Core Object Model focuses on:

- The concepts necessary to describe object interfaces: concepts are described from the server's point of view, rather than from the client's.

- The concepts required to describe software: the Core Object Model does not address interactions with hardware, multimedia flows, and ODP streams or capsules.

- The minimal set of concepts, which are needed to provide a basis for full software operation.

The Core Object Model does not provide specifications for object behavior; in other words, the implementation of objects is not specified. Instead, it provides a model for the specification of behavior. A description of behavior would require the definition of a formal semantics and is currently outside the scope of this document.

4.4 Description of the Core Object Model

This section describes the following concepts of the Core Object Model:

- Objects
- Operations, including signatures, parameters, and return values
- Non-object types

- Interfaces

- Substitutability

- Types, including information about subtyping and inheritance

- The relationship between CORBA and the Core Object Model

4.4.1 Objects

An object can model any kind of entity or concept; for example, a person, a ship, a document, a department, an order transaction, a tuple, a file, a window manager, or a lexical scanner. A basic characteristic of an object is its distinct object identity, which is immutable, persists for as long as the object exists, and is independent of the object's properties or behavior.

4.4.2 Operations, Signatures, Parameters, and Return Values

This section speaks in terms of "operations being applied to objects." This same concept can be described as "sending requests to objects." For the purpose of the Core Object Model, the two phrases mean the same thing.

Operations are provided by an object. Thus, to determine a person's date of birth, the **date_of_birth** operation is applied to the appropriate **person** object. The relationship between a person and his/her spouse may be modelled as an operation **spouse** on one person object, which returns another person object.

Each operation has a signature. A signature consists of the operation's name, set of parameters, and set of results. (Note that in the Core Object Model, the term *parameter* is used when referring to the declaration of an operation's interface. *Argument* is used when referring to an operation invocation.)

In the Core Object Model, operations (definitions of signatures) are not objects. Requests (operation invocations) are also not objects.

An example of a signature is shown in Code Example 4-1. Keep in mind, however, that the Core Object Model does not describe the syntax of an operation specification. For instance, it does not specify how results are to be associated with variables.

```
operation_name (param-1, ..., param-n)
    returns (res-1, ..., res-m)

param-i ::= parameter_name: parameter_type
res-i ::= result_name: result_type
```

Code Example 4-1   Sample Syntax of a
Signature

In its simplest form an operation need not have parameters and need not return a value.

Each of the operations on an object should have a unique name. The only exception is in C++, where in some cases parameters signify differences.

An operation describes an action that can be applied to parameters. An operation invocation, called a *request*, (like a procedure invocation or function call) indicates an operation, can list some parameters on behalf of a requester (client), and can cause the operation to return results. The consequences of a request can include the following:

- An immediate set of results

- Side effects, manifested in changes of state

- Exceptions (currently not part of the Core Object Model) indicating that some unusual event has occurred and passing that information to an exception handler

All operations defined on an object type have distinct names. In the object model, an operation is defined on a single object type, so there is an operation that cannot be independent of an object type, or be defined on two or more object types. Requiring operations to be defined on a single type is sometimes referred to as the classical object model: the Core Object Model is a classical object model. (Allowing operations to be defined on zero or more types is called the generalized object model.)

In the Core Object Model, operations can only be defined on object types, not on non-object types.

An operation can have side effects. The model does not distinguish a subcategory of operations that are free of side effects.

The Core Object Model does not address exception handling. Exceptions are intended to be introduced as a component and can therefore be included in profiles.

The Core Object Model does not specify anything about the execution order for operations. For example, whether clients issue requests sequentially or concurrently is not part of the model. Furthermore, whether requests get serviced sequentially or concurrently is also not part of the model. In short, it neither specifies nor precludes an implementation from supporting sequential or concurrent operations.

The Core Object Model neither requires nor precludes support for atomic operation execution. An implementation might choose to provide atomic operations instead of separate **transaction_begin, transaction_commit,** and **transaction_abort** operations.

The Core Object Model does not require a formal specification of the semantics of an operation, although it is good practice to include a comment that specifies the purpose of the operation, any side effects it has, and any invariance it is intended to preserve.

4.4.3 Non-Object Types

Many object systems, for example C++ and CORBA-compliant systems, explicitly distinguish between objects and things that are not objects. The Core Object Model recognizes this distinction. Things that are not objects are called *non-objects*. Examples of non-objects are the basic and constructed values as defined in the CORBA specification.

Objects and non-objects collectively represent the set of denotable values. In the Core Object Model, non-objects are not labelled by an object reference. The Core Object Model does not specify a set of non-object types; these types are defined in a component and chosen for inclusion in a profile. For example, CORBA defines in its profile that the non-object types include: Short, Long, UShort, Ulong, Float, Double, Char, String, Boolean, Octet, Enum, Struct, Sequence, Union, and Array. The set of non-object types can be extended by adding new types to the Non-object component.

Profiles can choose which non-object types to support. In a pure object system, such as Smalltalk, all denotable values are expressed as objects, so the set of non-object types may be empty. Thus profiles are allowed to make the difference between the set of objects and set of non-objects that they recognise as either wide or narrow, as needed.

The set of all non-object types is called *NTypes*. The set of all non-objects is called *Nobj*. The complete set of values that may be manipulated in the Core Object Model is described as

$$DVal = Obj \cup Nobj$$

DVal can be thought of as the denotable values in the Core Object Model.

The elements of *DVal* are called *dvals*. *DVal* is not a type in the core object model. It does not exist as a supertype of *Object* and the types in *NTypes*. Therefore, you cannot specify, for example, an operation parameter that may be either an object or a non-object. This eliminates the difficulty of systems having to provide runtime discrimination of objects and non-objects.

4.4.4 Interfaces and Substitutability

Unless otherwise noted, when this section refers to type, it means object type.

The Core Object Model is a classical object model: invocations are directed to a single target object. Each invocation includes an operation name and a set of parameters, and returns a set of results. The Core Object Model does not encompass exceptions, multiple terminations from operations, or multiple result values per operation.

If a client attempts to invoke an operation not supported by an object, or to invoke an operation with the wrong type or number of parameters, or receives back results which differ in number or type from those which the client can use, an *interaction error* is said to have occurred. By comparing the names and signatures of the operations offered by an object with those the client may try to invoke, it is possible to predict interaction errors.

A collection of operation signatures is termed an *interface*. Operations within an interface are distinguished by name: an interface may not contain two operations with the same name. Interfaces are related to each other by substitutability relationships. Interface A is *substitutable* for interface B if a client that expects to use an object presenting interface B can get and use a reference to an object with interface A. This must occur without an interaction error. There are many valid substitutability relationships. A common one allows an object to be used anywhere that the client requires an interface comprising a strict subset of the operations in the supplied object's interface, so that the operations that the client could invoke are present with exactly the signatures required. Although the supplied object may also support other operations, this support does not affect the correct operation of the client. Such a relationship is sometimes termed an *extension relationship*.

As can be seen, a valid substitutability relationship is not necessarily symmetrical. If A is substitutable for B, it does not necessarily hold that B is substitutable for A. However, substitutability is transitive: if A is substitutable for B, and B substitutable for C, then it follows that A is substitutable for C.

4.4.5 Types

Although an object can be substituted for another object that presents the same interface without causing an interaction error, the operation bodies that will be invoked by calling the operations may not necessarily perform appropriate functions. Even if there is no interaction error, a client may nevertheless invoke operations in a sequence or with parameter values that are not meaningful to the object, thus causing *application errors* in the object. Similarly, the behavior of the object may not match the client's expectations. Hence, substitutability of interfaces is a necessary, but not sufficient, condition for determining whether one object can be used in place of another.

The other factors to consider when determining substitutability are diverse and potentially much less well-defined than the interface.

They may include notions of ownership, behavior, remuneration, and implementation. The Core Object Model does not directly address these issues, but simply uses the term *type* to cover the union of the interface plus all the other properties of an object that determine whether it is suitable for a particular purpose. The non-interface aspects of types are not explicitly represented in the Core Object Model. A type consists of an interface and a programmer-asserted relationship to one or more other types. This assertion is implicit in the way that a new type is constructed through *inheritance*.

4.4.6 Inheritance and Subtyping

When an object of type A is substitutable for an object of type B, A is said to be a subtype of B, and B a *supertype* of A.

In the Core Object Model, all new types are specified in terms of existing types using inheritance. Inheritance in the Core Object Model is defined so that every type constructed by inheriting from another is automatically one of its subtypes. A type is defined to be a subtype of any type in the transitive closure of types from which it inherits, and is not a subtype of any type outside this transitive closure.

Although the Core Object Model effectively defines its inheritance to be the same as subtyping, the two concepts must be considered to be separate. Subtyping determines substitutability, whereas inheritance is a mechanism for specifying one entity in terms of another. Other object systems have different inheritance mechanisms that apply to implementations (rather than types), and do not produce implementations that are substitutable for those from which they inherited. By the same token, substitutability is possible between entities that have no inheritance relationship. Smalltalk's inheritance mechanism is a good example of one that is completely unrelated to subtyping or substitutability. Defining subtyping in terms of construction (inheritance) rules has shortcomings in object systems that cross enterprise boundaries, since separate enterprises cannot separately create the same type (so that their applications can work together). Yet since they may be in competition, neither would be happy to use a type that was somehow "owned" by another enterprise.

Another shortcoming is that a new type must be defined as a subtype of an existing type, not as a supertype. This problem can usually be solved by inferring the subtype relationship by examining types, rather than having designers and programmers assert them[*].

---

[*] The Emerald distributed programming language uses this approach; see *Emerald: a General Purpose Programming Language*, Black et al, Software: Practice and Experience, January 1991.

4.4.7 Inheritance Rules for the Core Object Model

Every object in the Core Object Model is a *direct instance* of one type. This type— called the *immediate type* of the object—is specified when the object is created. The object presents an interface that is the same as that specified in the immediate type, and is substitutable for all other instances of the immediate type and instances of its supertypes but no others, even if the interfaces of the types are substitutable. The set of direct instances of a type is called its *extension.* Note that the extension of a type need not necessarily be represented, or even knowable, in an implementation of the Core Object Model, since the objects in a distributed object system may be created and destroyed quite rapidly.

The Core Object Model mandates a single type with no operations. It is the ultimate supertype of all other types and is called *Object*[*].

In the Core Object Model every type is defined by inheriting from a set containing at least one other previously defined type. Every operation in the interface of every member of this set automatically

---

[*]An alternative name, used in some systems, is *Any.* Some object type systems introduce the complimentary *None* type that is substitutable for all others. If a programming language has a NIL element that is substitutable for any other value then its type (whether explicitly defined or not) is *None.* It is impossible to write the type *None*, since it must have all possible operations, each with all possible cardinalities and sets of parameter types. It must therefore be built in.

becomes an operation in the interface of the new type. If any two of these operations have the same name but different signatures, the set is inconsistent and cannot be used. The designer may specify additional operations for the interface provided that none has the same name as an inherited operation. These inheritance rules automatically construct a new type that is a subtype of all the types from which it inherits. Note that the Core Object Model does not have an explicit reference to type of self, nor does it allow redefinition of operations. If it did, these inheritance rules would not generate subtypes.

Every non-object is an instance of a *non-object type*. Non-object types do not belong to the object type hierarchy; there is no substitutability between any object type and any non-object type.

Although terms such as type, operation, and interface are defined, there need not be objects representing any of these at runtime in a system that implements the Core Object Model.

4.4.8 Graphs and Hierarchies

In any type system, the types and their subtype relationships form a directed graph. Since in the Core Object Model new types are defined only in terms of previously defined types, its subtype graph is actually a *tree* or *hierarchy*. There are no pairs of types which are mutually substitutable, and every pair of types has at least one common ancestor for which they are both substitutable (even if it is only *Object*). Furthermore, there is one type in this set of supertypes that is a subtype of every other member of the set; this property makes the Core Object Model type graph a particular form of hierarchy called a *semi-lattice*.

4.5 Relationship to CORBA

What the Core Object Model calls a type, CORBA calls an interface. CORBA has no separate term for a collection of operations separated from an inheritance relationship. The CORBA interface inheritance rule is slightly more restrictive than that of the Core Object Model: no type can inherit an operation with the same name from more than one supertype.

The CORBA specification discusses the use of inheritance to construct new interfaces by extending existing ones; substitutability is not addressed. Most ORB implementors have interpreted this to mean that an object is only substitutable for another if its interface inherits—directly or indirectly—from the other's interface, and not otherwise.

In addition, the CORBA specification has exceptions, which are part of an operation's signature. Exceptions are not defined in the Core Object Model.

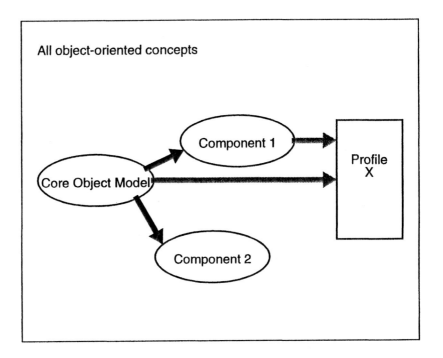

Figure 4-1 Ideas Underlying the Core Object Model

CHAPTER 5

Reference Model

5.1 Purpose of the Reference Model

This chapter describes the Reference Model for the Object Management Architecture (OMA). The Reference Model forms a conceptual road map for assembling technology that satisfies the OMG's Technical Objectives (see Chapter 3). It has three intended audiences:

- The OMG itself. The Reference Model provides a framework for guiding the process of soliciting and evaluating distributed object management technology.

- Potential technology providers. The Reference Model provides an architectural structure for positioning and presenting proposed technology in relation to others.

- Application developers and the software industry in general. The Reference Model articulates the OMG's vision for highly interoperable applications and services using object technology.

Though the Reference Model is intended to influence the high-level architectural and component designs of proposed approaches, it also accommodates a variety of different design solutions. The function of the Reference Model is more to map out areas to be addressed than to impose design constraints, except at the highest architectural level. The Reference Model identifies and characterizes the components, interfaces, and protocols that compose the OMG's Object Management Architecture, but does not itself define them in detail. It puts in place a structure that allows requirements to be defined and solutions to be proposed; it provides a framework that the OMG can populate with detailed interface and protocol specifications. (All OMG specifications are evaluated and approved by the membership of the OMG. The procedures that are used to evaluate and approve specifications are explained in Appendix B.)

The specifications that have been, to date, accepted by the OMG and its membership are described in "Associated Documents," on page 13.

In addition to providing the framework for writing specifications, the Reference Model:

- Identifies the major separable components of the total Object Management Architecture. The components are: Object Request Broker, Object Services, Common Facilities, and Application Objects.

- Characterizes the functions provided by each component.

- Explains the relationships between the components and with the external operating environment.

- Identifies the protocols and interfaces for accessing the components.

Specifically, the Reference Model addresses:

- How objects make and receive requests and responses.

- The basic operations that must be provided for every object.

- Object interfaces that provide common facilities useful in many applications.

5.2 Object Management Architecture

An application that is "OMA-compliant" consists of a set of inter-working classes and instances that interact via the ORB (as defined in the next section). Compliance therefore means conformance to the

OMA and the protocol definitions and ORB enables objects to make and receive requests and responses.

- The Object Request Broker is the central component of the Object Management Architecture and is the key to interoperability. It allows invocation of operations on objects distributed around a network without regard to the networking software, operating system, or application that implements those objects. Specifications for an OMG-compliant ORB are contained in *CORBA: Common Object Request Broker Architecture and Specification.*

- Object Services is a collection of services with object interfaces that provide basic functions for realizing and maintaining objects. Specifications for Object Services are contained in *CORBAservices: Common Object Services Specification.*

- Common Facilities is a collection of classes and objects that provide general purpose capabilities useful in many applications. Specifications for Common Facilities are contained in *CORBAfacilities,* which will be published in 1995.

- Application Objects (AO) are specific to particular end user applications.

In general, the Application Objects and Common Facilities have an application orientation while the Object Request Broker and Object Services are concerned with the "system" or infrastructure aspects of distributed object management. Common Facilities may, however, provide higher-level services, such as transactions and versioning, that use primitives provided by Object Services.

Of the four Reference Model components, three lend themselves to standardization: Object Services, Common Facilities, and Common Object Request Broker. Thus, they will be the focus of OMG standardization efforts. The fourth component, Application Objects, represents functions that are too specialized to standardize at this time.

In general, Object Services, Common Facilities, and Application Objects all communicate using the Object Request Broker. Objects may also use non-object interfaces to external services, but these are outside the scope of the OMA. Although not explicit in the Reference Model, objects may (or may not) communicate with the Object Services via object interfaces. For example, the addition of a new class may be cast as a request to an object that provides this service, but equivalently, it could be performed by editing a class definition script or a C++ include file.

The Application Objects and Common Facilities use and provide functions and services via object interfaces. Objects can issue and process requests. Thus, objects categorized as Application Objects can provide services for other applications or facilities. For example, an application specific service such as printer rendering could be cast as an application object invoked by a common facility such as a print queue. Equally, objects categorized as Common Facilities may use services provided elsewhere.

Common Facilities exemplifies a key concept that the OMA promotes, class reusability.

It is important to note that applications need only provide or use OMA-compliant interfaces to participate in the Object Management Architecture. They need not themselves be constructed using the object-oriented paradigm. This also applies to the provision of Object Services. For example, existing relational or object-oriented database management systems could be used to provide some or all of the Object Services. Figure 5-2 on page 96 shows how existing applications, external tools, and system support software can be embedded as objects that participate in the Object Management Architecture, using class interface front-ends (otherwise called *adapters* or *wrappers*).

The Reference Model does not impose any restrictions on how applications and common facilities are structured and implemented. Objects of a given application class may deal with the presentation of information, interaction with the user, semantics, functionality, the persistent storage of data, or a combination of the above.

The OMA assumes that underlying services provided by a platform's operating system and lower-level basic services, such as network computing facilities, are available and usable by OMA implementations. Specifically, the Object Management Architecture does not address user interface support. The interfaces between applications and windowing systems or other display support are the subjects of standardization efforts outside the OMG. Eventually, however, Common Facilities may provide standard user interface classes. In addition, the Reference Model does not deal explicitly with the choice of possible binding mechanisms (e.g., compile time, load time, and runtime).

The following sections describe each part of the OMA in more detail. It should be noted that the partitioning of functionality, particularly between Object Services and Common Facilities, represents a "best guess" and can be expected to evolve as different design approaches are evaluated and the Reference Model is refined.

5.3 Object Request Broker (ORB)

The Object Request Broker (ORB) provides the mechanisms by which objects transparently make and receive requests and responses. In so doing, the ORB provides interoperability between applications on different machines in heterogeneous, distributed environments and seamlessly connects multiple-object systems.

The specifications for an OMA-compliant ORB are contained in *CORBA: Common Object Request Broker Architecture and Specification.*

The Core Object Model (see Chapter 4) defines an object request and its associated result (response) as the fundamental interaction mechanism. A request names an operation and includes zero or more parameter values, any of which may be object names identifying specific objects. The ORB arranges for the request to be processed. This entails identifying and causing some method to be invoked that performs the operation using the parameters. After the operation terminates, the ORB conveys the results to the requester.

The ORB itself might not maintain all of the information needed to carry out its functions. In the process of conveying a request, the ORB may generate requests of its own to Object Services, or otherwise use them. For example, in order to find the specific method to be executed for a given request, the ORB might use a class dictionary service or might search runtime method libraries.

In order to satisfy the OMG Technical Objectives, the ORB is expected to address all of the following areas, at least to some degree.

- Name services. Object name mapping services map object names in the naming domain of the requester into equivalent names in the domain of the method to be executed, and vice versa. The OMG Object Model does not require object names to be unique or universal. Object location services use the object names in the request to locate the method to perform the requested operation. Object location services may involve simple attribute lookups on objects. In practice, different object systems or domains will have locally preferred object naming schemes.

- Request dispatch. This function determines which method to invoke. The OMG Object Model does not require a request to be delivered to any particular object. As far as the requester is concerned, it does not matter whether the request first goes to a method that then operates on the state variables of objects passed as parameters, or whether it goes to any particular object in the parameter list.

- Parameter encoding. These facilities convey the local representation of parameter values in the requester's environment to equivalent representations in the recipient's environment. To accomplish this, parameter encodings may employ standards or de facto standards (e.g., OSF/DCE, ONC/NFS/XDR, NCA/NCS/NDR, ASN.1).

- Delivery. Requests and results must be delivered to the proper location as characterized by a particular node, address, space, thread, entry point. These facilities may use standard transport protocols (e.g., TCP/UDP/IP, ISO/TPn).

- Synchronization. Synchronization primarily deals with handling the parallelism of the object's making and processing a request and the rendezvousing of the requester with the response to the request. Possible synchronization models include: asynchronous (request with no response), synchronous (request; await reply), and deferred synchronous (proceed after sending request; claim reply later).

- Activation. Activation is the housekeeping processing necessary before a method can be invoked. Activation and deactivation ("passivation") of persistent objects is needed to obtain the object state for use when the object is accessed, and save the state when it no longer needs to be accessed. For objects that hold persistent information in non-object storage facilities (e.g., files and data-bases), explicit requests can be made to objects to activate and deactivate themselves.

- Exception handling. Various failures in the process of object location and attempted request delivery must be reported to requester and/or recipient in ways that distinguish them from other errors.

Actions are needed to recover session resources and resynchronize requester and recipient. The ORB coordinates recovery house-keeping activities.

- Security mechanisms. The ORB provides security enforcement mechanisms that support higher-level security control and policies. These mechanisms ensure the secure conveyance of requests among objects. Authentication mechanisms ensure the identities of requesting and receiving objects, threads, address spaces, nodes, and communication routes. Protection mechanisms assure the integrity of data being conveyed, and assure that the data being communicated and the fact of communication are accessible only to authorized parties. Access enforcement mechanisms enforce access and licensing policies.

As an example of the function of the ORB, consider the request **print layout_312 laser_plotter**. This could be sent to the **object layout_312** whose print method would then print it on **laser_plotter**. Or the request could be sent to **laser_plotter** whose print method would access **layout_312**. Or the request could be sent to a general-ized print routine that would figure out a good way to arrange the printing, based on some attributes of these two objects. Or, instead of relying on a generalized print routine, the Name Service in the ORB could determine an appropriate method jointly owned by (the classes of) **layout_312** and **laser_plotter**.

5.3.1 *Common Object Request Broker Architecture Specification*

In September 1991, the OMG selected a standard interface for the ORB component of the Object Management Architecture. This ORB standard, adopted from a joint proposal of Digital Equipment Corporation, Hewlett Packard Company, HyperDesk Corporation, NCR Corporation, Object Design Inc., and SunSoft Corporation, is called CORBA. It is outlined in detail in *CORBA: Common Object Request Broker Architecture and Specification.* In 1992, the CORBA specification was revised. In 1995, the CORBA specification was again updated to support the following items:

- Mappings to the C++ and Smalltalk programming languages

- Extended interface repositories

- Portable initialization procedures

- Full Object Request Broker interoperability, including transaction-ing and security

The most important feature of any CORBA specification is its Interface Definition Language (OMG IDL). The OMG IDL language is used by applications to specify the various interfaces they intend to offer to other applications via the ORB layer. Application may make use of this interface specification information to access local or remote services in both a static fashion (high-performance, compile-time, optimized), or dynamically (with much greater flexibility).

5.4 Object Services

Object Services provides basic operations for the logical modeling and physical storage of objects.

Object Services defines a set of intrinsic or root operations that all classes should implement or inherit. Objects do not have to use the implementation of basic operations provided by Object Services, nor do objects have to provide all basic operations. For example, an object may provide its own data storage; an object that models a "process" may not provide transactions.

The operations provided by Object Services are made available through the ORB. Object Services may also be made available through other interfaces. For example, there may be additional interfaces that comply with non-OMG standards or that are optimized for higher performance. Stated differently, Object Services does not impose a single implementation or interface, rather, it defines at least one interface that can be used regardless of an object's realization and regardless of other interfaces provided by the infrastructure.

The operations provided by Object Services can serve as the building blocks for extended or augmented functionality provided by Common Facilities. For example, Object Services can provide transaction management that spans objects, implementations, and machines. Certain aspects of a function can more easily be provided by software that is intrinsically concerned with controlling an object, while the more generalized, abstract, or multi-object implementation of a function can be better provided by Common Facilities.

The operations that Object Services can provide include:

- Class management. The ability to create, modify, delete, copy, distribute, describe, and control the definitions of classes, the interfaces to classes, and the relationships between class definitions.

- Instance management. The ability to create, modify, delete, copy, move, invoke, and control objects and the relationships between objects.

- Storage. The provision of permanent or transient storage for large and small objects, including their state and methods.

- Integrity. The ability to ensure the consistency and integrity of object state both within single objects (e.g., through locks) and among objects (e.g., through transactions).

- Security. The ability to provide (define and enforce) access constraints at an appropriate level of granularity on objects and their components.

- Query. The ability to select objects or classes from implicitly or explicitly identified collections based on a specified predicate.

- Versions. The ability to store, correlate, and manage variants of objects.

The types of subcomponents that could be used to implement Object Services include object-oriented database management systems, transaction managers, query facilities, directory services and file services.

5.4.1 Object Services Specification

Specifications for Object Services typically consist of a set of OMG IDL interface definitions (syntax) and a description of operation behavior and request sequencing (semantics). Specifications for the following Object Services are contained in the *CORBAservices* manual:

- Naming

- Event

- Life Cycle (including Compound Life Cycle)

- Persistent Object

- Transaction

- Concurrency Control

- Relationships

- Externalization

5.4.2 Summary of Object Services

This section provides a brief description of each Object Service.

The Naming Service provides the ability to bind a name to an object relative to a naming context. A naming context is an object that contains a set of name bindings in which each name is unique. To resolve a name is to determine the object associated with the name in a given context. Through the use of a very general model and in dealing with names in their structural form, Naming Service implementations can be application specific or be based on a variety of naming systems currently available on system platforms.

Graphs of naming contexts can be supported in a distributed, federated fashion. The scalable design allows the distributed, heterogeneous implementation and administration of names and name contexts.

Because name component attribute values are not assigned or interpreted by the Naming Service, higher levels of software are not constrained in terms of policies about the use and management of attribute values.

The Event Service provides basic capabilities that can be configured together flexibly and powerfully. The service supports asynchronous events (decoupled event suppliers and consumers), event "fan-in," notification "fan-out,"—and through appropriate event channel implementations—reliable event delivery.

The Event Service design is scalable and is suitable for distributed environments. There is no requirement for a centralized server or dependency on any global service. Both push and pull event delivery models are supported; that is, consumers can either request events or be notified of events.

Suppliers can generate events without knowing the identities of the consumers. Conversely, consumers can receive events without knowing the identities of the suppliers. There can be multiple consumers and multiple suppliers of events. Because event suppliers, consumers, and channels are objects, advantage can be taken of performance optimizations provided by ORB implementations for local and remote objects. No extension is required to CORBA.

The Life Cycle Service defines services and conventions for creating, deleting, copying, and moving objects. Because CORBA-based environments support distributed objects, life cycle services define services and conventions that allow clients to perform life cycle operations on objects in different locations. The client's model of creation is defined in terms of factory objects. A factory is an object that creates another object. Factories are not special objects. As with any object, factories have well-defined OMG IDL interfaces and implementations in some programming language.

The Life Cycle Service also supports compound life cycle operations on groups of related objects.

The Persistent Object Service (POS) provides a set of common interfaces to the mechanisms used for retaining and managing the persistent state of objects. The object ultimately has the responsibility of managing its state, but can use or delegate to the Persistent Object Service for the actual work. A major feature of the Persistent Object Service (and the OMG architecture) is its openness. In this case, that means that there can be a variety of different clients and implementations of the Persistent Object Service, and they can work together. This is particularly important for storage, where mechanisms useful for documents may not be appropriate for employee databases, or the mechanisms appropriate for mobile computers do not apply to mainframes.

The Transaction Service supports multiple transaction models, including the flat (mandatory in the specification) and nested (optional) models. The Transaction Service supports interoperability between different programming models. For instance, some users want to add object implementations to existing procedural applications and to augment object implementations with code that uses the procedural paradigm. To do so in a transaction environment requires the object and procedural code to share a single transaction. Network interoperability is also supported, since users need communication between different systems, including the ability to have one transaction service interoperate with a cooperating transaction service using different ORBs.

The Transaction Service supports both implicit (system-managed transaction) propagation and explicit (application-managed) propagation. With implicit propagation, transactional behavior is not specified in the operation's signature. With explicit propagation, applications define their own mechanisms for sharing a common transaction.

The Transaction Service can be implemented in a TP monitor environment, so it supports the ability to execute multiple transactions concurrently, and to execute clients, servers, and transaction services in separate processes.

The Concurrency Control Service enables multiple clients to coordinate their access to shared resources. Coordinating access to a resource means that when multiple, concurrent clients access a single resource, any conflicting actions by the clients are reconciled so that the resource remains in a consistent state.

Concurrent use of a resource is regulated with locks. Each lock is associated with a single resource and a single client. Coordination is achieved by preventing multiple clients from simultaneously possessing locks for the same resource if the client's activities might conflict. Hence, a client must obtain an appropriate lock before accessing a shared resource. The Concurrency Control Service defines several lock modes, which correspond to different categories of access. This variety of lock modes provides flexible conflict resolution. For example, providing different modes for reading and writing lets a resource support multiple concurrent clients on a read-only transaction. The Concurrency Control service also defines Intention Locks that support locking at multiple levels of granularity.

The Relationship Service allows entities and relationships to be explicitly represented. Entities are represented as CORBA objects. The service defines two new kinds of objects: *relationships* and *roles*.

A role represents a CORBA object in a relationship. The Relationship interface can be extended to add relationship-specific attributes and operations. In addition, relationships of arbitrary degree can be defined. Similarly, the *Role* interface can be extended to add role-specific attributes and operations. Type and cardinality constraints can be expressed and checked: exceptions are raised when the constraints are violated.

The Life Cycle Service defines operations to copy, move, and remove graphs of related objects, while the Relationship Service allows graphs of related objects to be traversed without activating the related objects. Distributed implementations of the Relationship Service can have navigation performance and availability similar to CORBA object references: role objects can be located with their objects and need not depend on a centralized repository of relationship information. As such, navigating a relationship can be a local operation.

The Externalization Service defines protocols and conventions for externalizing and internalizing objects. Externalizing an object is to record the object state in a stream of data (in memory, on a disk file, across the network, and so forth) and then be internalized into a new object in the same or a different process. The externalized object can exist for arbitrary amounts of time, be transported by means outside of the ORB, and be internalized in a different, disconnected ORB.

For portability, clients can request that externalized data be stored in a file whose format is defined with the Externalization Service Specification.

The Externalization Service is related to the Relationship Service and parallels the Life Cycle Service in defining externalization protocols for simple objects, for arbitrarily related objects, and for facilities, directory services, and file services.

5.4.3 Common Facilities (CF)

Common Facilities comprises facilities that are useful in many application domains and which are made available through OMA-compliant object interfaces. Unlike Object Services, which will be supported on all platforms, Common Facilities is optional. Not all standardized facilities will be available on all platforms, but, if available, they will provide the OMG approved semantics.

For application developers, Common Facilities reduces the effort needed to build OMA-compliant applications. For example, an OMA-compliant CAD schematic editor could use a common OMG Help facility to provide end-user help. In addition, application developers may define subclasses to enrich or customize the functionality of Common Facilities for specific applications.

For end users, Common Facilities provides uniform semantics that are shared across applications, making OMA-compliant applications easier to use.

A service becomes a Common Facility when it:

- Communicates using the ORB

- Implements a facility that OMG chooses to adopt

- Has an OMA-compliant object interface

The following list shows the Common Facilities that have been identified by OMG and its membership as candidates for the Common Facilities category:

User Interface Common Facilities

- Rendering management (such as printing and display)

- Compound presentation mangement (such as printing and display in compound documents)

- User support facilities (such as text checking)

- Desktop management (facilities for end user desktop)

- Scripting (interactive creation of automation scripts)

Information Management Common Facilities

- Information modeling

- Information storage and retrieval

- Data interchange and compound data interchange

- Information exchange

- Data encoding and representation (data format encodings and translations)

- Time operations (manipulation of calendar and time data)

Systems Management Common Facilities

- Management tools (interoperability of such tools)

- Collection management (integration of collection management facilities and managed objects)

- Control facilities (control of system resources and managed objects)

Task Management Common Facilities

- Workflow (coordination of objects in a work process)

- Agent (supporting static and dynamic agents)

- Rule management (knowledge acquisition, maintenance, execution of rule-based objects)

- Automation (access to functionality of one object from another object)

Vertical Market Facilities, including facilities for imagery, information, CIM, distributed simulation, oil and gas industry exploitation and production, accounting, application development, and mapping.

5.5 Application Objects (AO)

The AO classification corresponds to the traditional notion of an application. Generally developed by VARs (Value-Added Resellers) and ISVs (Independent Software Vendors), AOs represent individual related sets of functionality (e.g., word processing and stock ticker display). The value of developing these applications inside OMA is the improved ability to wed that single-minded functionality with other classes. The ability to integrate application classes also extends to the integration of traditional, extant, non-object–oriented applications within the same framework. Thus an existing spreadsheet product could be fully integrated into an OMA-compliant system using embedding.

It is important to realize that classes that fall into the AO classification are at the same OMA semantic level as CF classes; the difference is that CF classes represent very common functionality (which is adopted by the OMG as a standard), while AO classes are more specialized, representing interfaces that are specific to an application

domain and not standardized by the OMG. However, specific applications may be structured along standards arising from other standards organizations such as ISO and ANSI.

An OMA-compliant application consists of a collection of interworking objects. Classes and objects may be used in multiple applications. For example, a given class could provide shared services,
perhaps specific to a particular application domain. Existing applications and data elements (files, databases, etc.) may be embedded in
classes and objects.

A long list of possible programs is expected to fall within the AO
classification, including:

- Office applications: word processing, spreadsheets, electronic
  mail, etc.

- CAD applications: EDA, ECAD, MCAD, CAE, architectural
  CAD, etc.

- CASE tools: programming support, database design tools, etc.

- Network management applications.

- Information access and query applications. The entire range of
  query systems would fall into the AO classification, including general database query, geographic information systems, reservation
  transaction systems, etc.

- Knowledge-based systems.

It is important to note that individual AO-classified classes can "migrate" into the CF classification if a commonality of interface becomes apparent. In addition, in new programs one might expect traditional applications to extend across boundaries; for instance, the query portion of a PC database product might be found in the AO classification in a port to a more OMA-oriented style.

Examples of possible requests in the AO classification include:

- **lookup_spreadsheet_cell(spreadsheet_object,cell_location)** to read and return the value of a cell in a spreadsheet object.

- **edit_ascii_text(editor_object,text_string)** to run a text editor on some text to be edited, allowing user interaction with an editing tool represented by an editor object.

- **query_database(query_object,sql_string)** to do database lookup through the good graces of an SQL-compliant database query processor.

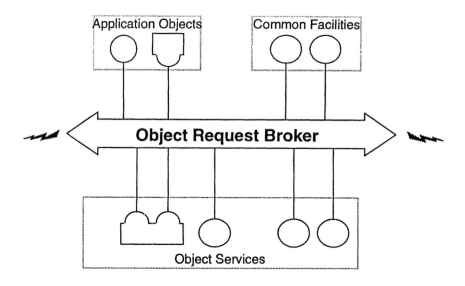

Figure 5-1   Reference Model: OMA
Overview.

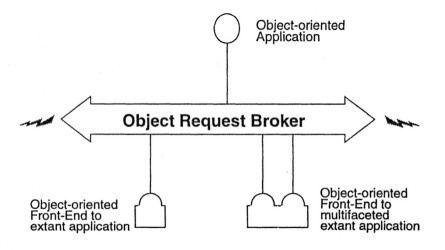

Figure 5-2   Wrapping Existing Applications

Glossary

This glossary contains terms used throughout this guide. Many of these terms are more specifically defined in Chapter 4 or Chapter 5. Text in *italics* is for clarification only.

For more information about object-oriented terminology, refer to the Semaphore *Glossary of Object-Oriented Terminology.* (Semaphore email: 74743.16@compuserve.com).

activation Copying the persistent form of methods and stored data into an executable address space to allow execution of the methods on the stored data.

application A dynamic object-based application is the (end-user) functionality provided by one or more programs consisting of a collection of interoperating objects. *In common terminology this is usually referred to as a running application or process.* A static object-based application is a set of related types and classes specific to a particular (end user) objective. *In common terminology this is usually referred to as a program.*

application facilities Comprise facilities that are useful within a specific application domain. See *common facilities*.

application objects Applications and their components that are managed within an object-oriented system. Example operations on such objects are open, install, move and remove.

asynchronous request A request where the client object does not pause to wait for results.

atomicity The property that ensures that an operation either changes the state associated with all participating objects consistent with the request, or changes none at all. If a set of operations is atomic, then multiple requests for those operations are serializable.

attribute A conceptual notion. An attribute of an object is an identifiable association between the object and some other entity or entities. Typically, the association is revealed by an operation with a single parameter identifying the object. See related definition for *property.*

behavior The behavior of a request is the observable effects of performing the requested service (including its results).

behavior consistency Ensures that the behavior of an object maintains its state consistency.

binding (or, more specifically, **method binding**) The selection of the method to perform a requested service and of the data to be accessed by that method. See also *dynamic binding* and *static binding*.

class An implementation that can be instantiated to create multiple objects with the same behavior. An object is an instance of a class. Types classify objects according to a common interface; classes classify objects according to a common implementation.

class inheritance The construction of a class by incremental modification of other classes.

class object An object that serves as a class. A class object serves as a **factory**. See *factory*.

client object An object issuing a request for a service. See also *server object. A given object may be a client for some requests and a server for other requests.*

common facilities Provides facilities useful in many application domains and which are made available through OMA-compliant class interfaces. See also *application facilities*.

component A conceptual notion. A component is an object that is considered to be part of some containing object.

compound object A conceptual notion. A compound object is an object that is viewed as standing for a set of related objects.

conformance A relation defined over types such that type x conforms to type *y* if any value that satisfies type *x* also satisfies type *y*.

context-independent operation An operation where all requests that identify the operation have the same behavior. (In contrast, the effect of a context-dependent operation might depend upon the identity or location of the client object issuing the request.)

core object model Basic object model that forms the basis for the OMG's Object Management Architecture; formally defined in Chapter 4 of this guide. The Core Object Model defines concepts such as object and non-object types, operations, signatures, parameters, return values, interfaces, substitutability, inheritance, and subtyping.

data model A collection of entities, operators, and consistency rules.

delegation The ability for a method to issue a request in such a way that self-reference in the method performing the request returns the same object(s) as self-reference in the method issuing the request. See *self-reference*.

dynamic binding Binding that is performed after the request is issued (see *binding*).

embedding Creating an object out of a non-object entity by wrapping it in an appropriate shell.

exchange format The form of a description used to import and export objects.

export To transmit a description of an object to an external entity.

extension of a type The set of values that satisfy the type.

factory A conceptual notion. A factory provides a service for creating new objects.

generalization The inverse of the specialization relation.

generic operation A conceptual notion. An operation is generic if it can be bound to more than one method.

handle A value that unambiguously identifies an object. See also *object name.*

implementation A definition that provides the information needed to create an object, allowing the object to participate in providing an appropriate set of services. An implementation typically includes a description of the data structure used to represent the core state associated with an object, as well as definitions of the methods that access that data structure. It also typically includes information about the intended type of the object.

implementation inheritance The construction of an implementation by incremental modification of other implementations.

import Creating an object based on a description of an object transmitted from an external entity.

inheritance The construction of a definition by incremental modification of other definitions. See also *implementation inheritance.*

instance An object created by instantiating a class. An object is an instance of a class.

instantiation Object creation.

interface A description of a set of possible uses of an object. Specifically, an interface describes a set of potential requests in which an object can participate meaningfully. See also *object interface, principal interface,* and *type interface.*

interface inheritance The construction of a new interface using one or more existing interfaces as its basis. The new interface is called a subtype and the existing interfaces are its supertypes.

interface type A type that is satisfied by any object (literally, by any value that identifies an object) that satisfies a particular interface. See also *object type.*

interoperability The ability to exchange requests using the ORB in conformance with the OMG Architecture Guide. *Objects interoperate if the methods of one object request services of another.*

link A conceptual notion. A relation between two objects.

literal A value that identifies an entity that is not an object. See also *object name.*

meaningful request A request where the actual parameters satisfy the signature of the named operation.

metaobject An object that represents a type, operation, class, method, or other object model entity that describes objects.

method Code that may be executed to perform a requested service. *Methods associated with an object may be structured into one or more programs.*

method binding See *binding*.

multiple inheritance The construction of a definition by incremental modification of more than one other definition.

non-object A member of the set of denotable values. Non-objects are not labeled by an object reference.

object A combination of a state and a set of methods that explicitly embodies an abstraction characterized by the behavior of relevant requests. An object is an instance of a class. *An object models a real world entity and is implemented as a computational entity that encapsulates state and operations (internally implemented as data and methods) and responds to requests for services.*

- A basic characteristic of an object is its distinct object identity, which is immutable, persists for as long as the object exists, and is independent of the object's properties or behavior.

- Methods can be owned by one or more objects.

- Requests can be sent to zero, one, or more objects.

- State data can be owned by one or more objects.

- State data and methods can be located at one or more locations.

object creation An event that causes an object to exist that is distinct from any other object.

object destruction An event that causes an object to cease to exist and its associated resources to become available for reuse.

object interface A description of a set of possible uses of an object. Specifically, an interface describes a set of potential requests in which an object can meaningfully participate as a parameter. It is the union of the object's type interfaces.

object name A value that identifies an object. See also *handle*.

object services A collection of interfaces and objects that support basic functions for using and implementing objects. Object Services are necessary to construct any distributed application and are independent of application domains. Interfaces for object services are specified by OMG in *CORBAservices* and currently include Life Cycle, Events, Naming, Persistent Object, Transaction, Concurrency Control, Relationships, and Externalization.

object type A type the extension of which is a set of objects (literally, a set of values that identify objects). In other words, an object type is satisfied only by (values that identify) objects. See also *interface type*.

OMA-compliant application An application consisting of a set of interworking classes and instances that interact via the ORB. Compliance therefore means conformance to the OMA protocol definitions and interface specifications outlined in this document.

OMG IDL Object Management Group Interface Definition Language. A programming language–independent way to specify object interfaces. OMG IDL must be used to specify all object interfaces in a CORBA-compliant system; it is used only for specifications, not for programming. The specification for OMG IDL is contained in *CORBA*.

operation A service that can be requested. An operation has an associated signature, which may restrict which actual parameters are possible in a meaningful request.

operation name A name used in a request to identify an operation.

ORB (Object Request Broker) provides the means by which objects make and receive requests and responses.

parameter Part of an operation's signature. It gives the type and name of an argument to the operation.

participate An object participates in a request if one or more of the actual parameters of the request identifies the object.

passivation The reverse of activation.

persistent object An object that can survive the process or thread that created it. A persistent object exists until it is explicitly deleted.

principal interface The interface that describes all requests in which an object is meaningful.

property A conceptual notion. An attribute the value of which can be changed.

protection The ability to restrict the client objects for which a requested service will be performed.

query An activity that involves selecting objects from implicitly or explicitly identified collections based on a specified predicate.

referential integrity The property that ensures that a handle which exists in the state associated with another object reliably identifies a single object.

request An event consisting of an operation and zero or more actual parameters. A client issues a request to cause a service to be performed. Also associated with a request are the results that may be returned to the client. *A message can be used to implement (carry) a request and/or a result.*

result The information returned to the client, which may include values as well as status information indicating that exceptional conditions were raised in attempting to perform the requested service.

security domain An identifiable subset of computational resources used to define security policy.

self-reference The ability of a method to determine the object(s) identified in the request for the service being performed by the method. (Self-reference in Smalltalk is indicated by the keyword *self*. See also *delegation*.)

server object An object providing response to a request for a service. See also *client object*. *A given object may be a client for some requests and a server for other requests.*

service A computation that may be performed in response to a request.

signature Defines the types of the parameters for a given operation.

single inheritance The construction of a definition by incremental modification of one definition. See also *multiple inheritance*.

specialization A class x is a specialization of a class y if x is defined to directly or indirectly inherit from y.

state The information about the history of previous requests needed to determine the behavior of future requests.

state consistency Ensures that the state associated with an object conforms to the data model.

state integrity Requires that the state associated with an object is not corrupted by external events.

state-modifying request A request that by performing the service alters the results of future requests.

state variable Part of the state of an object.

static binding Binding that is performed prior to the actual issuing of the request. See also *binding*.

supertype When an object of type A is substitutable for an object of type B, A is a subtype of B, and B is a supertype of A. Although the Core Object Model effectively defines its inheritance to be the same as subtyping, the two concepts are separate. Subtyping determines substitutability, whereas inheritance is a mechanism for specifying one entity in terms of another.

synchronous request A request where the client object pauses to wait for completion of the request.

transient object An object the existence of which is limited by the lifetime of the process or thread that created it.

type A predicate (Boolean function) defined over values that can be used in a signature to restrict a possible parameter or characterize a possible result. Types classify objects according to a common interface; classes classify objects according to a common implementation.

type interface Defines the requests in which instances of this type can meaningfully participate as a parameter. *Example: given that document type and product type the interface to document type comprises edit and print, and the interface to product type comprises set price and check inventory, then the object interface of a particular document which is also a product comprises all four requests.*

type object An object that serves as a type.

value Any entity that can be a possible actual parameter in a request. Values that serve to identify objects are called "object names." Values that identify other entities are called "literals."

value-dependent operation An operation where the behavior of the corresponding requests depends upon which names are used to identify object parameters (if an object can have multiple names).

Policies and Procedures of the OMG Technical Committee

This appendix outlines the policies and procedures used by the Technical Committee of the Object Management Group, Inc. These policies and procedures may change by vote of the Technical Committee as the needs and purpose of the Technical Committee change.

> Sections set off from the text in the manner of this section are explanations or *rationales*, and are not actually a part of this document. Rather, they reflect the rationale and reasoning behind a decision laid out in the *Policies and Procedures* in order to better reflect the intent of the document.

B.1 Purpose of the Technical Committee

The bylaws of the Object Management Group state that, *"The Technical Committee shall be responsible for developing, proposing, and publicizing definitions, standards, extensions, and proposing resolution of issues relevant to the OMG Core Technology and its use in conjunction with both hardware and software."* We interpret this statement to be a directive to design a *reference model* (or abstract architecture) for an object-oriented application environment, and then use this architectural reference to solicit, propose, review, recommend modifications to, and recommend adoption of technology. Specific proposed technologies are manifested by *Items* before the TC, which go through the procedures outlined in Section 4 for potential recommendation of adoption.

> It should be clear from the Bylaws of the OMG that the TC is designed to be a consulting body, making recommendations only to the BOD. The BOD makes all final decisions of the OMG.

B.2 Definitions and Acronyms

- **OMG.** The Object Management Group.
- **BOD.** The OMG Board of Directors, as defined by the bylaws of the OMG.

- **TC**. The OMG Technical Committee, composed of individuals duly appointed by the BOD to be members of the Committee.

- **TCC**. The Technical Committee Chair, a post held by the Vice President and Technical Director of the OMG, to lead the activities of the TC.

- **Item**. Questions and issues before the committee for discussion, resolution and final recommendation to the BOD. The *Items* are tracked and numbered by the TCC. Items come about through TC membership motions and seconds, typically in response to RFPs, BOD directives, TF recommendations, or the normal course of TC business.

- **OMG Member, or Member**. Any member in good standing of the OMG with membership class other than Subscriber.

- **OMG Corporate Member, or Corporate Member**. A corporate member in good standing of the OMG.

- **TC Member**. Any member of the TC.

- **Voting TC Member**. Any member of the TC who may vote on TC items. Voting TC Members represent OMG Corporate Members or the End User Membership; only one representative from a given member company may be a Voting TC Member, and only one representative from all of the End User Member companies (the End User Voter) may be a Voting TC Member.

- **Invited Guest.** A liaison representative appointed by an external organization which has reciprocal liaison status with the OMG, or an individual who has received at least two invitations to attend meetings of the TC. Invitations may only be issued by Corporate Members or the End User Voter. It is the policy of the OMG to freely allow guests and observers to attend meetings. To attend a meeting, guests and observers must request permission from the OMG.

- **OMG End User Member, or End User Member.** An end user member in good standing of the OMG.

- **End User Voter.** An elected representative of all end user member companies who may vote in the TC and subcommittees.

- **Subcommittee, or SC.** A standing group of individuals composed of members of the TC and invited guests, with a general portfolio to provide recommendations to the TC in some area.

- **Subcommittee Chair, or SCC.** An individual member of a SC responsible for leading the activities of a SC, as well as presenting SC recommendations to the TC.

- **Task Force, or TF.** A group of individuals composed of members of the TC and invited guests, with the specific purpose of solving some particular problem or problems in a particular arena for recommendation to the TC. A particular use of the Task Force structure is to generate Requests for Information or Proposals, and to evaluate responses. A Task Force is *not* a subcommittee as outlined by the Bylaws of the OMG.

- **Task Force Chair, or TFC**. An individual member of a TF responsible for leading the activities of a TF, as well as presenting TF recommendations to the TC.

- **Special Interest Group, or SIG**. A group of individuals composed of members of the TC and invited guests with a general area of interest outside the immediate goals of the TC. Typically a SIG is formed to explore specific technology areas and generate OMG Discussion Papers in that topic area. A Special Interest Group is *not* a subcommittee as outlined by the Bylaws of the OMG.

- **Special Interest Group Chair, or SIGC**. An individual member of a SIG responsible for leading the activities of a SIG, as well as presenting SIG Discussion Papers to the TC, and to the TCC for distribution by the OMG.

- **Request for Information, or RFI**. A general request to the computer industry to submit information to one of the TC's TFs detailing companies' current or planned offerings in a particular technology.

- **Request for Proposals, or RFP.** An explicit request to the computer industry to submit proposals to one of the TC's TFs. Such proposals must be received by a certain deadline (see Section 4.2) and are evaluated by TFs.

- **Proposed Technology.** Technology in the form of an existing, operational implementation that an OMG Corporate Member wishes to sponsor under the Bylaws of the OMG in response to an RFP. *Proposed Technology* is evaluated by the TC for potential recommendation as *Sponsored Technology*.

- **Sponsored Technology.** Technology that has been sponsored by an OMG Corporate Member, and proposed and accepted as Sponsored Technology under the OMG Bylaws, e.g., by the BOD.

   The definition of a *Task Force* is motivated by a wish to remove from these working groups the need to conform to the Bylaws-mandated Corporate Member-only voting policy. TF structure and voting, as outlined in Section 3.8, is more liberal than that required for committees and subcommittees of the OMG. The terminology *Sponsored Technology,* for what might be better called *Accepted Technology*, is culled directly from the Bylaws for compatibility.

B.3 Policies of the Technical Committee

As noted in the definition of the Technical Committee, the TC is appointed by the BOD. However, the Technical Committee should have the following composition:

- The Technical Committee Chair (a direct representative of the OMG itself)

- Representatives of all members of the OMG

- Other individuals deemed appropriate by the BOD

Although each member of the OMG may be represented in Technical Committee meetings by individuals, only OMG Corporate Members may send Voting TC members to TC meetings (and only one Voting TC Member may vote on behalf of each OMG Corporate Member). There is no limit to the number of TC members that may represent each OMG member company at TC meetings, although the TCC may limit the number of attendees (on a maximum-per-company basis) for reasons of meeting space, and so on. The TCC shall be responsible for forming a recommendation to the BOD listing the suggested members of the TC for appointment by the Board.

B.3.1 Meetings of the Technical Committee

Technical Committee meetings shall be conducted under the general guidance of *Robert's Rules of Order.* Meetings shall be conducted by the TCC or another appointed representative of the OMG. Meetings shall occur approximately every eight weeks. Meetings must be announced, by paper, at least four weeks in advance. Minutes of TC meetings shall be distributed by paper within two weeks of the meeting.

> By "paper" this document means by the regular international postage system, or by facsimile machine. Electronic mail shall be used by the TC and its members, but certain important communications (such as TC meeting notification and TC minutes) shall be delivered by more positive means.

B.3.2 Attendance at Technical Committee Meetings

Only members of the TC and Invited Guests are welcome at meetings of the TC. Guest lecturers may appear on meeting dates, but no TC business may be transacted while other than TC members and Invited Guests are present. Any TC member may send another representative of his or her company as a substitute to a TC meeting.

B.3.3 Agenda of a Technical Committee Meeting

The agenda for a TC meeting shall be determined at the end of the previous meeting. The agenda is managed solely by the TCC, and may be modified prior to the meeting as appropriate, as long as notice requirements of the different phases of the technology adoption procedure are met. A written agenda shall be distributed to TC members at least two weeks before each TC meeting.

> In order to allow the business of the TC to move along smoothly, the TCC may adjust the agenda based on members' schedules, available presentations and meeting sites, etc. Members are protected from capricious agenda changes by requirements for lead time on procedural presentation and votes.

B.3.4 Voting During and Between Technical Committee Meetings

A simple majority of Voting TC Members whose companies have attended, in person or through proxy, two of the last three TC meetings, shall constitute the quorum necessary for the TC to conduct business. A simple majority of the Voting TC Members present at a meeting shall constitute a proper vote on all TC Items, *except* on changes to these Policies and Procedures, or on final BOD recommendation votes, q.v., "Procedures for Adoption of Proposed Technology," on page 136. A two-thirds (2/3) vote of attending Voting TC Members is required to change these Policies and Procedures; in addition, the vote to change these Policies and Procedures must be announced in the preliminary agenda of the meeting.

> In order to avoid deadlocking TC business through the continued lack of attendance of Corporate Members, it was felt that some flexibility in the definition of quorum was necessary. This quorum policy, in which only one half of consistently attending Member companies are required for quorum, protects active Members and the TC process as a whole, without ever depriving Corporate Members of a vote.

Voting Members may send substitutes to TC meetings, but these substitutes may only vote with a written proxy statement by the Voting TC Member of his or her company. A paper (postal or facsimile) vote by a Voting TC Member may also be accepted at a TC meeting.

> In order to ensure that business moves along, we wish to allow proxy voting, duly noting the dangers of voting without physical proximity. We feel that the notification requirements for the different phases of technology sponsorship sufficiently protect member companies from adoption without due ability to oppose.

The Technical Committee Chair may not vote in TC votes, except in a tie-breaking capacity during an otherwise deadlocked majority vote. In regard to votes that require documentation (i.e., on adoption of particular documents or based on the content of a document), one third of the Voting TC members in attendance may invoke the requirement that documentation supporting the vote must be available three weeks prior to the vote.

> The three-week rule clause ensures that Voting TC members will have adequate time to read, distribute, and gather comments on documents before voting on the document at the following TC meeting.

The End User Voter will be selected by the End User Member companies by majority vote of the End User Special Interest Group, and announced by that SIG to the TC whenever such End User Voter is elected. In the event the End User SIG becomes defunct (has not met in one year), it will be deemed that there is no End User Voter.

The TC can take votes by fax between TC meetings. Fax votes may be brought by motion and second at a TC meeting, or by direct action of the TCC. Quorum for a fax vote shall be equal to a majority of the number of Voting TC Members whose companies have attended, in person or by proxy, at least one of the last three TC meetings at the time that the fax vote is initiated. Fax votes may be withdrawn by simple majority vote of the TC at a TC meeting.

Fax votes shall terminate, on a date approved by the TCC, no less than six weeks and no more than ten weeks after the date that the fax voting forms are sent (by fax) to Voting TC Members. If a quorum of voters (as defined by the fax voting quorum rule above) has not returned voting forms by the deadline, the vote will be deemed to have failed. The vote will not be considered complete until either (1) the deadline has been reached and the quorum rule has been satisfied, or (2) no further votes received could change the outcome of the vote.

It is often necessary to obtain votes between TC meetings; fax quorum rules simplify the requirements for such voting. Since an incomplete fax vote might be aborted at a TC meeting and retaken (with meeting quorum rules!), it was suggested that the TCC include in each TC fax vote wording to the effect: "(COMPANY) votes (YES NO ABSTAIN) on fax question #X. If this fax vote is withdrawn and a vote taken on the question at a TC meeting, I hereby give my proxy to vote this same way at the TC meeting on the question(s)."

B.4 Role of the Technical Committee Chair

The TCC is responsible for the continued progress of the Technical Committee. The TCC is an unbiased member of the TC, and therefore does not vote on Items (other than in the tie-breaking capacity mentioned in Section 3.5). The TCC shall ensure the following:

- Note is taken of TC Members, Voting TC Members, and their substitutes and proxies at each meeting.

- Minutes are kept of TC meetings, and distributed, by paper, within two weeks of the meeting.

- TC meetings are announced with appropriate notice (no less than four weeks) and agendas are published at least two weeks prior to each meeting.

- TC meetings are facilitated in general.

- A file of TC meeting minutes and all other distributed materials is kept.

- A file is kept for each Item that is under consideration by the TC.

- All electronic mail discussions are kept on file.

- The BOD is kept informed of the current business of the TC.

- TC resolutions for recommendation to the BOD are brought to the attention of the BOD.

- RFIs and RFPs are issued in a timely, orderly manner.

B.5 Working Groups of the Technical Committee

In order to carry out the business of the TC in a timely manner, three different types of working groups of the TC may be formed. These groups are called Subcommittees (SCs), Task Forces (TFs), and Special Interest Groups (SIGs). Each is composed solely of TC members and sometimes Invited Guests. Each type of group is created by simple majority vote of the TC in the course of regular business.

There are differences, however, between the types of groups. Subcommittees, for example, as described in the Bylaws of the OMG:

- Have corporate-member-only voting policies.

- Tend to meet only during TC meetings.

- Make non-standardization recommendations to the TC.

- Tend to deal with procedural or other non-standards issues.

- Set their own missions and goals.

In contrast to Subcommittees, Task Forces:

- Have all-member voting policies.

- Generally meet more often than the entire TC.

- Make standardization (adoption) recommendations to the TC.

- Deal primarily with standards issues.

- Have missions and goals defined by the TC.

Special Interest Groups are somewhere in between the other two types of groups, because they:

- Have all-member voting policies (except for the End User SIG, see "Special Interest Groups," on page 133).

- Tend to meet during TC meetings, although they may meet more frequently.

- Make no recommendations to the TC, but present Discussion Papers for distribution by the OMG.

- Deal primarily with non-standards issues.

- Define their own missions and goals.

> The purpose of this separation of types of groups is based on the three needs for working groups within the TC: standing groups to deal with procedural and definitional tasks; single-purpose groups to work on particular technology adoption questions; and wide-interest groups not in the mainstream of the immediate goals of the TC. Subcommittees fulfill this first goal, and guarantee Corporate Member control via their voting strategy. Task Forces fulfill the second goal, as outlined in the next section. Special Interest Groups provide a meeting place for companies interested in object technology questions not in the immediate mainstream of TC tasks, while allowing a

voice (discussion papers) that may be used to influence future standards.

The Policies and Procedures subcommittee will provide a list to the TC at least once a year of those Subcommittees and Special Interest Groups that have not met in the previous 12 months. The TC will then vote to determine if these groups should be continued, disbanded or possibly combined with more active groups.

In the past, some groups have not met for a considerable time and are no longer active. The existence of these groups can be misleading to those trying to understand what OMG is currently doing. This proposal suggests a mechanism for reviewing Subcommittees and Special Interest Groups and taking some action when appropriate. This will help ensure the groups in OMG are aligned with the actual work being done within the TC.

B.5.1 Membership in TC Subgroups

The following rules apply to membership in subgroups of the TC:

- Any OMG member company above the Subscriber grade may send representatives to attend any meeting of the TC or any sub-group of the TC, even if membership in that group has been closed.

Object Management Architecture Guide

- Task Forces may close their voting memberships, but are not required to do so (except in the case of Revision Task Forces, see "Post-Adoption Processes," on page 144). The reasons for closing a Task Force include delineation of quorum and voters for voting reasons, and avoidance of late vote-packing in the TF.

- Observers (representatives of companies that are not members of a Task Force) may actively participate at the sole discretion of the Task Force Chair. That is, in the interests of ensuring the efficient operation of any meeting, the TFC may limit or eliminate the opportunity of any observer to participate in discussion at any meeting.

- In order to close Task Force membership, Task Forces must announce the deadline for membership requests a minimum of twelve weeks in advance, to the entire Technical Committee. Any OMG member filing a Letter of Intent (LOI) with the OMG to submit technology in response to a Request for Proposal (RFP) will be automatically registered as a TF voter for that RFP.

B.6 Task Forces

In order to move quickly on technology adoption Items, most Items shall be referred to Task Forces. TFs have three general duties:

- Form a mission statement describing the purpose of the TF, for authorization by the TC. This mission shall of course be strongly influenced by the TC's intent in creating the TF. A TFC must come forward during this process to manage the affairs of the TF.

- Issue recommendations to the TC to issue Requests for Information and/or Proposals (RFIs and RFPs), which represent requests to the entire computer industry to fill portions of the abstract reference model of the TC.

- Evaluate proposed technologies of responses to RFPs, and recommend to the TC action to be taken in regard to these responses (e.g., acceptance, rejection, and conditional acceptance). Also evaluate possible modifications to existing sponsored technology, and recommend adoption of such modifications to the TC.

  Although only OMG Corporate Members may sponsor proposed technology for adoption by the TC (and thence by the BOD), RFPs are issued *to the industry*. This process allows the OMG to promulgate the best available technology for adoption. In order for a company that is *not* an OMG Corporate Member to sponsor a technology to the TC, that company must follow one of two paths: (1) the company may become a Corporate Member; or (2) the company may license the technology to an OMG Corporate Member that wishes to become the sponsor, under terms considered favorable to the availability of the technology (e.g., X/Open terms and conditions). This procedure balances the wish to welcome the *best* available technology, with the requirement of OMG control of the technology and the interests of the OMG member companies.

Task Forces without technology portfolios may also be formed to investigate certain other questions and make recommendations to the TC.

Such non-technology Task Forces might include standing TFs to handle questions related to open definition questions, such as the Ad Hoc task forces formed to write this and other sections of the *Object Management Architecture Guide.*

Voting in TFs is by majority of TC Members on the TF, not just Voting TC Members, with the caveat that no OMG member company may cast more than one vote in a TF vote. Quorum in Task Forces shall be defined as a simple majority of the number of official members of the TF which have attended two of the last three meetings of the TF co-located with TC meetings. TF votes on recommendations to the TC shall occur only in TF meetings co-located with TC meetings, or by facsimile.

It was felt that TFs should be able to use all of the expertise at hand in arriving at recommendations. All TC member companies could be represented (and *vote*) at TF meetings in order to allow the expression of all members' opinions. OMG Corporate Members are protected from control by non-Corporate members by virtue of the fact that TFs may only form recommendations to the TC, not final TC votes. TF minutes are also available to *all* members of the TC, so that other TC members may understand and accept or reject TF recommendations.

Only Task Forces may recommend issuance of a Request for Information or Request for Proposals by the TC, to avoid confusion in the industry as to the purpose of an OMG Request. Other subgroups (notably Special Interest Groups) may wish to issue industry-wide surveys similar to RFIs, leveraging the staff public relations and marketing capabilities of the OMG. These shall be labelled Surveys, and they are still subject to TC approval for issuance.

B.6.1 Role of a Task Force Chair

The Task Force Chair (TFC) of a Task Force is responsible for the activities of his or her Task Force, including:

- Recognizing the Members and Voting Members of the TF.

- Ensuring that minutes of TF meetings are taken, and made available within one week of the meeting electronically to the TCC for electronic transmittal to all TC members.

- Presenting TF recommendations and commentary to the TC.

- Keeping the TCC apprised of the progress of the TF.

- Developing and announcing meetings, and then facilitating those meetings.

- Organizing TF meetings so that they occur at locations which are geographically convenient for the membership.

- Encouraging broad participation of the TF membership.

B.6.2 Subcommittees

The structure of Subcommittees is exactly that of Task Forces, except that SCs have chartered Corporate-only voting. As for TFs, each OMG Corporate has only one vote per SC. Subcommittees are long-standing entities with general portfolios. SCCs have the same duties to their SCs as TFCs to TFs.

B.7 Special Interest Groups

The structure of Special Interest Groups is similar to that of Task Forces, with the same voting structure. Special Interest Groups shall often be used to hear presentations in their interest areas, as well as to generate discussion papers for the industry covering those technology areas. While these discussion papers shall be distributed by the

OMG, and might in fact lead to adopted standards later, they do *not* represent the official position of the OMG TC or the OMG itself. Each discussion paper distributed by the OMG shall include a cover page with the following statement: *This paper presents a discussion of technology issues considered in a Special Interest Group of the Object Management Group Technical Committee. The contents of this paper are presented to create discussion in the computer industry on this topic; the contents of this paper are not to be considered an adopted standard of any kind. This paper does not represent the official position of the Object Management Group nor that of the OMG Technical Committee.*

The End User Special Interest Group will be treated differently. As it is intended to provide End User Member input into the OMG TC processes, only End User Members may vote in the End User SIG. In addition, the End User SIG is charged with selecting the End User Voter.

B.8 Documents and Distribution

Three channels shall be used for discussion and distribution of documents within the TC. Electronic mail shall be used for day-to-day discussion and *unofficial* dissemination of documents to be viewed by

the TC. Paper (international post and facsimile) shall be used for all
official document dissemination to the TC; the TCC shall be responsible for numbering and/or naming such documents and keeping a file
of all such distributed documents. "Paper" form shall also include
diskettes with documents in electronic form, such diskettes to be
made available by international post. The format of such electronic
dissemination shall be determined by the TCC from time to time; at
this writing the standard formats will be PC-formatted 1.44MB diskettes with ASCII, Rich Text format and Postscript file formats.
Paper versions of all documents shall be stored and available from
OMG headquarters.

> It was felt that electronic mail, as it exists today, is a
> proper medium for discussion, but not a reliable medium
> for important documents. Therefore, documents shall
> remain in paper or electronic form, distributed by post.
> Documents are filed at OMG headquarters (under the purview of the TCC) in order to be fully available to current
> and future TC members.

B.9 Procedures for Adoption of Proposed Technology

This section describes the procedures for proposing technology to the OMG, and how the OMG evaluates and accepts that technology.

B.9.1 Technology Proposed for Adoption

Only Corporate Members of the OMG may propose technology for adoption as OMG standards to become sponsored technology. Proposed technology that is recommended to the OMG Board for acceptance must have an existing and operational implementation. Once a proposed technology is assigned an Item number, it is managed within the TC through the process described in "Steps to Technology Adoption," on page 138. The recommendation to the BOD of proposed technology for acceptance, or modification of sponsored technology, requires a vote of two-thirds (2/3) of all non-abstaining Voting TC Members, not just those members present at a TC meeting. Only companies who were Voting Members at the time the technology adoption vote started may vote in a technology adoption vote. If a Member loses its Voting status after a technology adoption vote has started, then (1) if that Member has already voted, the vote stands; but (2) if that Member has not already voted, then a vote of Abstain is entered for that Member. Lack of a vote does not count as a vote of Abstain; only a written vote of Abstain counts as such a vote.

> It was felt that this most important vote of all of the TC should be of the entire Voting TC membership, rather than a portion of a meeting quorum, to allow all OMG Corporate Members to have control over the issue. Note that the TCC may never cast a vote in this procedure, as the TCC vote may only be used for tie-breaking in simple majority votes.

It is the policy of the TC that proposed technology resulting from an RFP evaluation may be recommended to the BOD for acceptance conditional on certain changes to the implementation, that the TC deems necessary, within a specified time frame. Recommended changes to proposed technology do not require a working implementation before they may be recommended to the BOD.

> This clause is entirely to allow the TC to vote for *conditional* acceptance of a proposed technology. This acceptance would be provisional, based only the timely completion of the TC's suggested changes in the technology.

TC recommendations for acceptance of proposed technology to become sponsored technology are always with the caveat that the board ensures that the technology's sponsor company is in a position to develop (or have developed for the sponsor company), commercialize, and license the technology and implementation. In addition, the TC recommends acceptance based only on the Board's finding that the sponsoring company make the technology available.

> It was felt that it is not within the TC's purview to determine the ability nor intent of an OMG member and technology sponsor to commercialize a technology. However, it was felt that the TC's work would be fruitless without such ability and intent. Therefore, recommendations to the BOD shall implicitly or explicitly include such caveats. Availability of technology may be ensured by the BOD by two routes: (1) guarantees in the form of contractual licensing agreement terms in an agreement between the sponsoring company and the OMG; or (2) transfer of the copyright to the technology to the OMG itself. The placing of the technology in the public domain by the sponsoring member was not deemed appropriate, as control would pass completely from the OMG membership.

B.9.2 Steps to Technology Adoption

Task Forces are responsible for generating and issuing RFIs and RFPs requesting information and proposals from industry. TFCs shall coordinate issuance of RFIs and RFPs with the TCC, who shall bring issuance of the request to a vote in TC meetings. The issuance of an RFI is intended only to gather information for the operation of the TC or for an upcoming adoption cycle. The steps from the issuance of an RFP to industry include the following meetings (meetings are held about eight weeks apart):

1. Issuance of RFP to industry; the termination date is at least twelve weeks from the issue date. The RFP must clearly state the deadline for letters of intent to respond, responses and all other relevant dates, and list all other requirements for responses. In addition, requirements of OMG membership level (e.g., only Corporate Members may propose technology for adoption) must be clearly spelled out in the RFP.

2. The TC goes about other business.

3. Presentation meeting. Four weeks prior to this meeting, presentation packages are sent to all TC members describing all of the responses to the RFP. All responses to the RFP issued in meeting one are presented by their sponsors to the TC during this meeting. The responses are then sent to the TF that issued the RFP. The TF begins deliberation on the responses to the RFP.

4. No earlier than this meeting, the TFC of the TF considering the responses to the RFP reports on the recommendation of the TF to the TC for adoption of a technology, potentially with modifications. The TFC should provide enough commentary of the TF's deliberations to allow intelligent choice by the Voting TC Members. Also no earlier than this meeting, the TC votes on recommending to the BOD adoption of the technology response, taking into account the recommendation of the TF.

> The procedure outlined above provides a minimum adoption process of about twenty-four weeks. Voting members are protected from adoption of technology that they wish to vote against by the four-week agenda rule. This foreshortened process allows the TC to adopt a particular technology quickly, though the procedure will generally take longer than four meetings.

Each company that intends to submit technology (respond to an RFP), whether individually or jointly with other companies, must submit a letter of intent to respond (LOI) to the OMG by the date specified in the RFP. Submissions from companies that have not provided letters of intent, will not be considered by the OMG.

All companies participating in the submission of technology to the OMG should be bound by the same set of OMG requirements.

RFPs typically require that LOIs provide a statement of a company's intention to meet the OMG's commercial availability requirements.

In order not to place undue constraints on companies working towards joint submissions, companies are not obliged to explain in the LOI whether their intended submission will be an individual submission or one done jointly with one or more other companies.

The issuance of RFIs and RFPs shall be accomplished by such means (which may include methods such as advertising, issuance of press releases, direct mailings and/or other actions, but with due regard to the budgetary limitations of the OMG) as are intended to bring the request to the attention of as wide and representative a percentage of the industry as possible (including non-members) and generate the most technically valuable and diverse response.

Companies sponsoring technology in response to a RFP shall bear the cost of transmitting the appropriate documents describing the technology to the TC membership, after assignment of a document number by the TCC. The OMG may provide this distribution service, with appropriate reimbursement by the sponsoring company.

B.9.3 Requirements for Requests for Information and Proposals

RFIs and RFPs must include:

- A statement of who may respond to the Request.

- A statement of who may respond to subsequent Requests. For example, the statement for an RFI should explain who can respond to the RFP that will be issued after responses to the RFI are received.

- A statement that responses may not include proprietary information.

- A stipulation that responses must include a waiver of copyright for unlimited duplication by the OMG, if copyright is held on the document.

- A stipulation that responses must include a limited waiver of copyright such as to allow OMG members to make up to fifty copies of the document for OMG review purposes only, if copyright is held on the document.

- A stipulation that responses must include a proof of concept statement.

Respondents should also be strongly encouraged to make their submissions in electronic form as well as paper form; the particular electronic form to be encouraged shall be decided from time to time by the TCC. The current preferred format is a PC-formatted 1.44MB diskette with files in ASCII, Rich Text format and/or Postscript file formats.

OMG specifications (and therefore RFP responses) may reference specifications from other organizations. Incorporating specifications by reference requires that the OMG specification clearly designate what portions of the other specification are referenced, the version of the other specification, a complete reference to the other specification, and complete information on how to obtain the other specification. Whenever possible, submitting organizations are asked to make available to the OMG the referenced specification in soft or hard copy form.

Companies must provide a proof of concept statement in RFP responses to explain the ways in which their specification has been demonstrated to be technically viable.

It is important for the TC to understand the technical viability of an OMG submission during the evaluation process. The technical viability has a lot to do with the state of development of the technology being submitted. This is not the same as commercial availability which is a OMG BOD consideration. Proof of concept statements can contain any information deemed relevant by the submitter.

Some examples might be:

- This specification has completed the design phase and is in the process of being prototyped.
- This specification has been in a beta test program for 4 months.
- This specification has been announced and is currently implemented in product xyz which has a customer base in excess of 500 users.
- This technology has been utilized in five products, all of which are in the final stages of testing.

The closure dates for RFIs and RFPs, including RFP re-submissions, must be at least 3 weeks before the TC or Task Force meeting at which the relevant submissions are to be first reviewed.

This reduces the risk that TC and Task Force members arrive at meetings to review proposals without having seen the submissions and provides time for the OMG to send papers to its members.

B.9.4 Post-Adoption Processes

After adoption of a technology by the OMG, it is necessary for the TC to control and maintain the technology for three reasons:

- Initial cleanup of the specification. After adoption of a specification, Revision *x.0*, it may be necessary to refine the specification into Revision *x.1* to make it more usable by readers.

- Revision/Change/Maintenance. By way of response to implementors against the adopted specification, the TC needs to respond to questions and comment in a timely, useful manner with minor revisions (Revision *x.y* becomes Revision *x.y+1*).

- Enhancement. Over time the changes to the adopted specification warranted by substantial changes in the state of the art may require reissuance of a new adopted technology in that area (Revision *x.y* becomes Revision *x+1.0*).

The first two processes, cleanup and revision, both lead to minor version-number Revisions of an adopted specification; the enhancement process leads to a major version-number Revision. The enhancement process takes place by a new Request for Information/Request for Proposals process reissued some time after the adoption of a technology.

Cleanup and revision, however, shall be handled by *Revision Task Forces* appointed by the TC at the time of adoption of a technology. These Revision Task Forces will review the specification, comment from members and the public on the specification, and generate new minor revisions of the specification for potential adoption by the TC. After recommendation of adoption of a specification by a technology Task Force or Revision Task Force, such Task Force will also submit to the TC a slate of members for future Revision Task Forces for that technology; this slate will include, at least

- A list of the OMG member company representatives to sit on the Revision Task Force
- The deadline for comment on the specification
- The deadline for operations of the Revision Task Force

The slate of member representatives to sit on a cleanup Revision Task Force should include at least representatives of all submitters whose technology was adopted, if those companies wish to hold a seat on the Revision Task Force. If the operational deadline of a Revision Task Force passes without a recommendation of a Revision of the adopted technology, the TC may of course extend the deadline or reopen the TF membership, as necessary. Revision Task Forces operate under the same rules as other Task Forces, except that Revision Task Force membership is closed as outlined here.

The potential worry of closing a Revision Task Force

membership too early is controlled by the fact that such Task Forces have dissolution deadlines. If this deadline is not met, the TC may in fact completely dissolve a given Revision TF and start over.

B.10 Fast-Track Request for Comments Procedure

In order to allow "fast-track" adoption of an interface, for which a Corporate Member has an acceptable commercially available implementation with no competition, there is a second path to technology adoption which may operate in parallel to and in lieu of the Request for Proposals procedure.

Any Corporate Member with technology that meets the following requirements may make an unsolicited submission of that technology to the TFC of the relevant Task Force for presentation to that TF for consideration through a Request for Comments.

The technology must:

- Be relevant to a current Task Force adoption plan

- Conform to all applicable OMG-adopted technologies

- Be available in a commercially available implementation

There are cases in which Corporate Members have an important relevant technology in place and commercially available and would like that technology to be recognized as a standard so that customers may comfortably use the interface of the technology. Unfortunately, in some of these cases, even though the technology is relevant, the implementation is acceptable and no competition for the technology is likely to arise, the interest level of the OMG TC membership will not necessarily be high enough to work on adoption in that area. The RFC procedure allows a fast-track adoption cycle for exactly this case, which also covers the potential for fast-track adoption of standards built by other standards organizations and consortia.

The steps are as follows:

1. Corporate Member submits to the TFC of the relevant Task Force an unsolicited proposal for adoption through the Request for Comments procedure. This proposal must include a rationale for how the proposal fits into that Task Force's plan of technology adoption; how the proposal meets current OMG adopted technology conformance; and how the proposal meets the commercial availability requirements of the OMG (just as any RFP response must answer these questions). The proposal must include a Letter of Intent to ensure commercial availability of the technology, again as in the RFP process.

2. Upon majority agreement of the Task Force which received the proposal, the TF may recommend issuance of the proposal by the OMG TC as an RFC.

3. Upon majority agreement of the TC, the proposal is issued by the OMG as an RFC. The comment period then opens. Simultaneously, the Letter of Intent is presented to the OMG Business Committee so that it may examine the proposal under its commercial availability criteria. The TC may decide not to issue the proposal for RFC for many reasons, including (but not limited to) the lack of perceived need for the technology; the likelihood of competition for the technology; the mismatch of the technology under the scopes of existing Task Forces; or simply that there are too many parallel Request processes under way at the time.

4. During the RFC period, any party (including all classes of OMG members, as well as any non-member of the OMG) may send comments on the proposal to OMG Headquarters, to an address announced with the RFC issuance. The OMG staff will

manage collection of the comments.

It is important that anyone may make a comment on an outstanding RFC, since there is no other public comment or response period for this technology. RFCs are to the industry, not just members (as are other Requests), and are publicized just as are other requests.

5. Ninety (90) days from issuance of the RFC, the RFC period closes. At this point, OMG staff makes a decision as to the significance of the received comment. If staff decides that the comment received was significant, the RFC "fails," adoption of the proposal halts and staff notifies the TC of the failure and reasons for failure. The TC may then follow the RFP approach to adoption in that area if it is deemed necessary. If, however, the comment received is deemed not to be significant, then the proposal is sent back to the TC for adoption recommendation with all comments received attached.

6. The TC then makes a final technology adoption decision with the usual two-thirds (2/3) voting margin to recommend the technology for adoption to the BOD.

B.11 Proprietary Rights

Proprietary information shall not be disclosed by any participant during any meeting of the OMG Technical Committee or any subgroup of the TC.

> This section clearly places the onus of protection of proprietary rights on the owner of those rights. No discussion of proprietary technology can take place during a TC or TC subgroup meeting, protecting the participants in the meeting from accidental exposure to proprietary information (and consequent future legal problems with that participant's own intellectual property rights). If a TC member wishes to present information of a proprietary nature to members of the TC, he or she may arrange a meeting of the interested parties totally separate from the TC process and meeting.

In addition, no information of a secret or proprietary nature shall be made available to the OMG as official documents, and no such documents (or documents marked as such) shall be made OMG official documents or forwarded to the membership.

All proprietary information which may nonetheless be publicly disclosed by any participant during any meeting of the OMG TC or any subgroup of the TC shall be deemed to have been disclosed on a nonconfidential basis, without any restrictions on use by anyone (except that no valid copyright or patent right shall be deemed to have been waived by such disclosure).

B.12 Adoption of This Document

In order to be accepted or modified, this document must be ratified by a two-thirds (2/3) vote (under the rules herein) at a TC meeting or via paper (e.g., postal or facsimile) vote. Changes to this document are to be presented to the TC, included in the meeting's minutes, and ratified by the same procedure. Meetings in which a vote on acceptance or modification of this document is to occur must include the change in the published agenda for the meeting. It is the responsibility of the TCC to get approval from the OMG counsel for any proposed change of these Policies and Procedures before the TC vote for adoption of that change.

B.13 Authorship and Revision

These Policies and Procedures initially were developed by the OMG TC Policies and Procedures Subcommittee, chaired by Dr. Richard Mark Soley of the Object Management Group. The revision history of the document is as follows:

Document 89-11-5 (November 8, 1989): First draft.

Document 89-12-2 (December 11, 1989): Adopted. Changes in adoption wording. Spelling corrected. Amendments per December 1989 TC meeting: Task Force chairs may vote; no proprietary conversations may be held at the TC meeting.

Document 90-2-17 (February 28, 1990): Amendment per February 1990 TC meeting: Documents must be available three weeks before vote.

Document 90-4-6 (April 12, 1990): Amendments per April 1990 TC meeting: meetings eight weeks apart rather than six, and separate Subcommittees, Task Forces, and Special Interest Groups.

Document 90-5-4 (May 17, 1990): Amendments per May 1990 TC meeting: quorum only majority of members who have attended two of the past three meetings, rather than majority of Corporate members. Two-thirds vote of quorum required to change Policies and Procedures.

Document 90-9-1 (September 4, 1990): Amendment per August 1990 TC meeting: three-week rule not automatic; instead may be invoked by one-third of quorum.

Document not published (March 1, 1991): Amendment per February 1991 TC facsimile vote: add provision for combined End User Member category voting.

Document 91-12-2 (December 23, 1991): Amendments based on November 1991 recommendations of Policies and Procedures Subcommittee, adopted at January 1992 TC meeting: allow distribution of electronic documents by post; add required statements to RFIs and RFPs; control Task Force membership; control evolution of adopted technology by revision and enhancement processes; add required legal purview over changes to Policies and Procedures; clarify non-member invited guest status; disallow proprietary document distribution; clarify facsimile voting rules.

Document 92-2-3 (February 11, 1992): Amendments adopted during January 1992 TC meeting: adoption of OMG counsel wording for observers, RFI issuance, and proprietary disclosure; encouragement of broad geographic representation at meetings.

Document 92-11-7 (November 23, 1992): Amendment adopted during October 1992 TC meeting: votes for changes to Policies and Procedures must be announced in meeting agenda.

Document 93-8-1 (August 2, 1993): Amendments adopted during July 1993 TC meeting: Request closure dates must allow time before

TC meetings; procedures to end dormant subgroups; extend Letter of Intent requirements to all cosubmitters; require statement of proof of concepts in Request responses.

Document 93-9-17 (September 24, 1993): Amendments adopted during September 1993 TC meeting: allow special voting procedures for End User Member companies.

Document 93-12-22 (December 15, 1993): Amendments adopted during December 1993 TC meeting: correct accidental disenfranchisement of End User Member companies; change Task Force quorum rules; change TC fax vote quorum rule and add time limitation to TC fax voting procedures; add Request for Comments fast-track adoption procedure.

Document 94-4-14 (April 13, 1994): Amendments adopted during April 1994 TC meeting: clarify fax voting rules; clarification of abstention and voting membership for technology adoption recommendation votes.

Document 95-1-48 (January 31, 1995): Amendment adopted during January 1995 TC meeting: automatically invite representatives of organizations with officially established liaison; allow End User Voter to invite guests.

Document 95-4-4 (April 26, 1995): Amendments adopted during March 1995 TC meeting: encourage availability of referenced documents; grant automatic Task Force voting membership for submitters.

Bibliography

[1] Bloor, Robin. **The Object Management Guide.** Butler Bloor Ltd., Challenge House, Sherwood Drive, Bletchley, Milton Keynes, MK3 6DP United Kingdom. Tel +1 44 908 373311, Fax +1 44 908 377470. April 1992.

[2] Booch, Grady. **Object-Oriented Design with Applications**. The Benjamin/Cummings Publishing Company Inc., Redwood City, CA. 1991.

[3] Burleson, Donald. **Practical Application of Object-Oriented Techniques to Relational Databases**. John Wiley & Sons, Inc., New York, NY. 1994.

[4] Cattell, Rick. **Object Data Management.** Addison-Wesley Publishing Company, Reading, MA. 1991.

[5] Cox, Brad. **Object-Oriented Programming, An Evolutionary Approach.** Addison-Wesley Publishing Company, Reading, MA. 1986-87.

[6] Fishman, D.H. et al. Iris: **An Object-Oriented Database Management System.** ACM Transactions on Office Information Systems, 5:1 (Jan. 1987).

[7] Hutt, Andrew. **Object Analysis and Design: Description of Methods**. John Wiley & Sons, Inc., New York, NY. 1994.

[8] Hutt, Andrew. **Object Analysis and Design: Comparison of Methods.** John Wiley & Sons, Inc., New York, NY. 1994.

[9] Keene, S. **Object-Oriented Programming in Common Lisp**. Symbolics Press and Addison-Wesley Publishing Company, Reading, MA. 1989.

[10] Kim, Won. **Object-Oriented Concepts, Databases, Applications**. Frederick Lochovsky. ACM Press Frontier Series. Addison-Wesley Publishing Company, Reading, MA. 1989.

[11] Kim, Won. **Introduction to Object-Oriented Data-bases.** MIT Press Computer Series, Cambridge, MA. 1990.

[12] Martin, James and Odell, James. **Object-Oriented Analysis and Design**. Prentice-Hall, Englewood Cliffs, NJ. 1992.

[13] Meyer, Bertrand. **Object-Oriented Software Construction**. Prentice Hall Publishing International Series in Computer Science. Englewood Cliffs, NJ. 1988.

[14] Snyder, A. **The Essence of Objects**. Report STL-89-25, Hewlett-Packard Laboratories, Palo Alto, CA, 1989.

[15] Taylor, David. **Managers Guide to Object-Oriented Technology**. Addison-Wesley Publishing Company, Reading MA.

[16] Winblad, Ann; Edwards, Samuel D; King, David R. **Object-Oriented Software**. Addison-Wesley Publishing Company, Reading, MA. 1990.

[17] Wirfs-Brock, Rebecca, Wilkerson, Brian, and Wiener, Laura. **Designing Object-Oriented Software.** Prentice Hall, Englewood Cliffs, NJ. 1990.

[18] Object Management Group. **CORBA: Common Object Request Broker Architecture and Specification.** Published by the Object Management Group (OMG), Framingham, MA. 1995.

[19]Object Management Group. **CORBAservices: Common Object Services Specification.** Published by the Object Management Group (OMG), Framingham, MA. 1995.

Index

T
Technical Committee 6, 114
Type 62
  Extension 64

Printed in the United Kingdom
by Lightning Source UK Ltd.
106221UKS00002B/187-206